Manufacturing
Human Bombs

Manufacturing Human Bombs

The Making of Palestinian Suicide Bombers

Mohammed M. Hafez

UNITED STATES INSTITUTE OF PEACE PRESS
Washington, D.C.

The views expressed in this book are those of the author alone. They do not necessarily reflect views of the United States Institute of Peace.

UNITED STATES INSTITUTE OF PEACE
1200 17th Street NW, Suite 200
Washington, DC 20036-3011

First published 2006

Printed in the United States of America

The paper used in this publication meets the minimum requirements of American National Standards for Information Science—Permanence of Paper for Printed Library Materials, ANSI Z39.48-1984.

Library of Congress Cataloging-in-Publication Data

Hafez, Mohammed M., 1970–
    Manufacturing human bombs: the making of Palestinian suicide bombers/
Mohammed M. Hafez.
        p. cm.
    Includes bibliographical references and index.
    ISBN-13: 978-1-929223-72-5 (softcover: alk. paper)
    ISBN-10: 1-929223-72-2 (softcover: alk. paper)
        1. Suicide bombings—Palestine. 2. Arab-Israeli conflict 1993- 3.
Political violence—Psychological aspects. 4. Terrorism—Government policy.
    I. Title.

HV6433.P25H34 2006

For Abeer, Omar, and Kareem

CONTENTS

FOREWORD

A Call for an Interdisciplinary Approach to Suicide Terrorism

Jerrold M. Post, M.D.

I n the spring of 1989, with the sponsorship of the Woodrow Wilson Center for International Affairs, Walter Reich organized a conference to explore "the psychological underpinnings of terrorist motivation and behavior." The participants' contributions were published the following year in a volume entitled *Origins of Terrorism: Psychologies, Ideologies, Theologies, States of Mind.* Reich initiated the conference with a debate, tasking Martha Crenshaw to marshal the arguments for terrorist behavior as a strategic choice, and tasking me to marshal the arguments that psychological processes undergird terrorist behavior. As Reich notes in the introduction to the book, he did this to emphasize that both approaches must be used to account for most instances and forms of terrorist behavior. Many readers of the volume apparently ignored the terms of reference for the debate spelled out in the introduction, for Crenshaw has been criticized for ignoring the psychological dimensions, while I have been criticized for ignoring the strategic logic of terrorist behavior.

Not constrained by Walter Reich, Mohammed Hafez has wisely taken an interdisciplinary approach in responding to the question whether it is strategic logic or other forces that underpin suicide terrorism by answering, both. He calls our attention to the complexity of the suicide terrorism phenomenon and insists on an interdisciplinary approach that takes into account three levels of analysis: individuals, organizations, and societies. He argues that there are at least three conditions required for suicide terrorism: a culture of martyrdom, a strategic decision to employ this tactic, and a political context that generates a supply of recruits.

That there are definitive elements of strategic choice seems clear. Just as Hezbollah, when celebrating Israel's withdrawal from southern Lebanon, made clear that it believed its violent campaign had worked, so too did Hamas, Islamic Jihad, and the al-Aqsa Martyrs Brigade claim credit amid the Palestinian celebrations of Israel's withdrawal from Gaza.

Yet while there is widespread support in the Palestinian territories for the strategic efficacy of the campaign of terror, especially suicide terror, by no means do all follow this pathway. What differentiates those who are attracted to this path from those who are not? Is the psychology of the Palestinian suicide bombers the same as that of the suicidal al Qaeda hijackers responsible for the coordinated attacks of 9/11? And what are the motivations of secular terrorist organizations, especially the Kurdish separatists of the PKK, the Tamil Tigers, and the Chechen nationalists?

Hafez has focused in this volume on Palestinian suicide bombers, but suggests that his overarching conclusions are applicable to suicide terrorism campaigns in other cultures as well, a conclusion with which I strongly agree. However, it is important always to locate each group accurately in its own political, historical, and cultural context.

One of the best ways of learning what makes terrorists tick is to ask them—which is why a number of us in the terrorism scholarship field have been interviewing terrorists for years. What was particularly striking about the population of incarcerated Middle Eastern terrorists my team interviewed in Israeli and Palestinian prisons was their apparent normality. The apparent paradox of how Islamic terrorists can commit suicide terrorism in the name of Allah when the Quran specifically proscribes suicide was succinctly resolved by one of the human bomb commanders we interviewed. Asked this question, he responded angrily, "This is not suicide. Suicide is weak; it is selfish; it is mentally disturbed. This is *istishad* [martyrdom or self-sacrifice in the name of Allah]."

Other pioneering scholars cited in this book have interviewed failed suicide terrorists to discover once again the apparent normality of the subjects. The terrorists emphasized that they were doing something for the cause of Palestinian nationalism, for their people, for the purpose of conveying to the weak and the powerless a sense of being able to do something. This was reminiscent of one of the subjects in our interview study, who, speaking of the positive value of being involved in this violent campaign, declared that "an armed action proclaims that I am here, I exist, I am strong, I am in control, I am on the field, I am on the map." This type of research needs to be expanded.

If the subjects are normal, without manifest psychopathology, how can we explain their willingness, indeed eagerness, to pursue this path? The answer is to be found in the sociocultural context and, for many, in the power of the destructive relationship between charismatic leaders and their followers. These hate-mongering leaders have an ability to connect with alienated, frustrated youth in such a manner that their individuality becomes subordinated to the collective identity, and they develop a willingness to sacrifice their individual lives if it serves the collective cause.

The power of the collective identity induced by the hypnotic influence of the destructive charismatic leader helps explain how the Tamil Tigers, a secular nationalist-separatist group, have so successfully adopted the strategy of suicide terrorism, for the suicide terrorists have yielded control of their lives to their powerful charismatic leader, Velupillai Prabhakaran. Indeed, although the LTTE is a secular group, its members ascribe near-Godlike status to Prabhakaran and uncritically accept his views and unquestioningly obey his directives.

While both the Palestinian suicide bombers and the suicidal hijackers of 9/11 kill in the name of God, they differ considerably. "Suicide autopsies"—the reconstruction of the lives of suicides—of the Palestinian human bombs in an Israeli study showed that they were conducted by young men in a rather narrow age range, 17–22 years of age (although recently that range has broadened, and both men and women have been involved). Unmarried, uneducated, and unemployed, they were unformed youth. The suicide bomb commanders emphasized to them their bleak prospects, that they could bring honor to their names, that they would be enrolled in the hall of martyrs, that their parents would be proud of them and would gain esteem in the community and receive financial benefits. Once a young man entered the safe house, he was never left alone lest he backslide, and he was physically escorted to the site of the bombing.

This stands in vivid contrast with the suicidal hijackers of 9/11, who were older (28–33 years of age with the exception of some younger individuals who were brought in late for "muscle" and who probably were unaware of the nature of the operation until it was under way) and well educated—Mohammed Atta and two of his colleagues were in a masters degree program in the technological university in Hamburg, and came from comfortable middle-class families in Saudi Arabia and Egypt. And, in striking contrast with the Palestinian suicide bombers, they had been on their own in the West, for as long as seven years, blending in with Western society while keeping within them like a laser beam their mission to give up their own lives while taking thousands of lives. They were fully formed adults who had subordinated their individuality to the cause of radical Islam as articulated by the destructive charismatic leader Osama bin Laden.

But for both groups it was the leaders, not the bombers themselves, who had made the strategic decision about the value of suicide terrorism—and those leaders seem unlikely to reverse that decision any time soon. As noted above, the withdrawal of Israel from the settlements in Gaza has confirmed for the leaderships of Palestinian terrorist groups the efficacy of their suicide bombing campaign.

The interdisciplinary approach that Hafez has advanced has important implications for countering this deadly strategy. The culture of martyrdom that he identifies is subject to very different interpretations by Muslim scholars, and moderate Muslim clerics have criticized the religious value of so-called "martyrdom operations" when the goal is killing innocents, emphasizing that the jihad of the sword is defensive, calling for taking up arms against those who take up arms against Muslims, and that there are plenty of Quranic and Prophetic sayings proscribing the killing of inno- cents: "Fight in the cause of God those who fight you, but do not transgress limits for God loves not the transgressor." But the voices of Muslim clerics challenging justifications for suicide terrorism have been all too muted, and need to be strengthened.

The organizational decision to employ suicide terrorism as a strategy is in part a strategy of desperation. Central to the IRA's decision to decom- mission its weapons was Sinn Fein's inclusion in the political process. Hamas has powerful support in the occupied territories and especially within Gaza. As Hamas enters and achieves representation within the political process, can this induce it to curtail its campaign of suicide terror- ism, as the IRA's inclusion led to a curtailment of its campaign of terror? And the third element specified by Hafez, a political environment that produces a ready supply of recruits, argues for a strategy to inhibit recruit- ment, a difficult strategy to devise to be sure, but one that would rest on providing alternative pathways for youth to succeed, for at present all too many frustrated and alienated Islamic youth see their only recourse as strik- ing out in despair.

Only by considering suicide terrorism in an interdisciplinary manner, as Hafez has done so well, can our understanding of this phenomenon be developed to serve as the foundation for an appropriate mix of interdisci- plinary tools to counter this deadly strategy. But it will be a long march, a long campaign, for at this time, for all too many, "hatred has been bred in the bone," and that attitude will not easily be countered.

ACKNOWLEDGMENTS

I would like to express my sincerest gratitude to the United States Institute of Peace for its generous grant toward this research project. I also want to thank Nicole Argo, Judy Barsalou, David Cook, Beverly Milton-Edwards, Assaf Moghadam, Ami Pedahzur, Jerrold Post, Nigel Quinney, Steven Riskin, Glenn Robinson, Marc Sageman, Anne Speckhard, Carrie Rosefsky Wickham, and the three anonymous reviewers for contributing in no small measure to the insights, arguments, and structure of this book.

NOTE ON DATA COLLECTION

T his book makes use of descriptive charts containing data on Palestinian suicide bombings since 1993, but especially since the second Palestinian uprising, which began in September 2000. I compiled the data on daily violent events between Palestinians and Israelis from September 1993 to February 2005 with the help of a team of graduate research assistants at the University of Missouri, Kansas City. The data were culled from the quarterly chronologies published in the *Middle East Journal*, which draws from several news sources, including the Associated Press, the BBC, the *New York Times*, the *Washington Post*, and many other reliable news services. We also collected data from the International Policy Institute for Counter-Terrorism (ICT) in Herzlia, Israel, which keeps detailed records of violent events in the second Palestinian uprising, and from LexisNexis searches using as our main sources *Ha'aretz* and *Jerusalem Post*, two Israeli daily papers that are published in English. Ancillary sources such as CNN and *New York Times* chronologies of suicide bombings in Israel and Israel's Ministry of Foreign Affairs chronologies of Palestinian attacks were used to provide more information on specific events, not as independent sources of data. The database is available for researchers upon written request to the author.

We encountered several challenges while collecting this data. First, we occasionally found discrepancies in news reports regarding the actual date of or number of persons killed or injured in an attack. In those instances we relied on Israeli sources because we assumed that they would have the most accurate information, given their stake in, and proximity to, the conflict. Second, in many instances initial reports of killed and injured were subsequently revised upward or downward by the authorities. When we became aware of those changes, we went back to revise individual entries in the database; however, we did not go back to verify every entry in the database, because of the time and effort required. Rarely do subsequent reports lead to substantial revisions in the number of killed or injured; rather, revisions typically result when one or two of those initially reported as injured die later from their injuries. Thus, our numbers of deaths and injuries may vary from those of other researchers or from those issued by Israel or the Palestinian Authority. Third, some events were difficult to categorize because of conflicting Palestinian and Israeli claims about what actually happened. For instance, some episodes deemed to be targeted assassinations by Palestinians are contested by Israelis as "workshop accidents"—that is, the militants blew themselves up while preparing an attack. When in doubt, we excluded these events from our database or used the category "unknown." As a result, our aggregate numbers may be substantially lower than what Palestinian and Israeli sources report. We recognize this limitation, but it is necessary in order to ensure the reliability of the data. Finally, our data capture those events that receive media attention. Many episodes of violence, such as random shootings and roadside bombings, go unreported, usually because they did not cause any casualties. Consequently, our data significantly underestimate the level of violence during the al-Aqsa uprising. Our aim is not to document each episode of violence but to reflect patterns in violence.

MANUFACTURING
HUMAN BOMBS

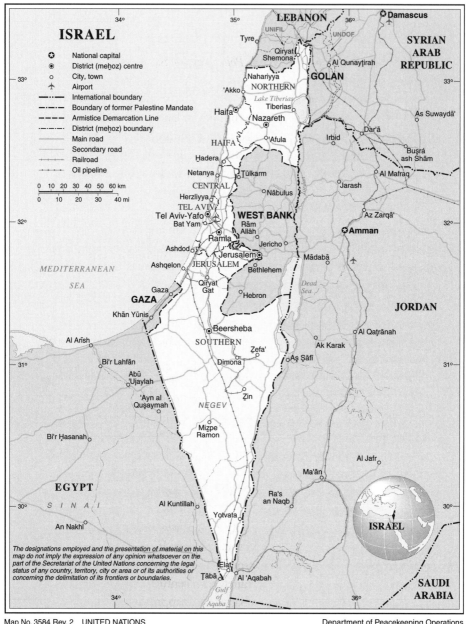

ISRAEL

❋ National capital
◉ District (meḥoz) centre
○ City, town
✈ Airport
▬ ▬ International boundary
▬ · ▬ Boundary of former Palestine Mandate
▬ ▬ ▬ Armistice Demarcation Line
▬ · ▬ District (meḥoz) boundary
Main road
Secondary road
┼┼┼┼ Railroad
┼┼┼┼ Oil pipeline

0 10 20 30 40 50 60 km
0 10 20 30 40 mi

MEDITERRANEAN
SEA

LEBANON
Tyre
UNIFIL
Qiryat Shemona
Nahariyya
'Akko
NORTHERN
Lake Tiberias
Haifa
Tiberias
Nazareth
HAIFA
'Afula
Ḥadera
Netanya
Ṭūlkarm
CENTRAL
Herzliyya
TEL AVIV
Tel Aviv-Yafo
Bat Yam
Rām Allāh
Ramla
Ashdod
Jerusalem
JERUSALEM
Ashqelon
Bethlehem
Gaza
Qiryat Gat
GAZA
Khān Yūnis
Hebron
Al ʿArīsh
Beersheba
SOUTHERN
Bi'r Laḥfān
Dimona
Abū ʿUjaylah
ʿAyn al Quşaymah
Zin
NEGEV
Bi'r Ḥasanah
Miẓpe Ramon

EGYPT
S I N A I
Al Kuntillah
An Nakhl
Yotvata
Ra's an Naqb
Maʿān
ʿElat
Ṭābā
Al 'Aqabah
Gulf of Aqaba

Damascus
UNDOF
Al Qunayṭirah
GOLAN
SYRIAN
ARAB
REPUBLIC
As Suwaydā'
Irbid
Darʿā
Buşrá
ash Shām
Jarash
Al Mafraq
Nābulus
WEST BANK
Az Zarqā'
Amman
Jericho
Mādabā
Dead Sea
JORDAN
Zefa'
Ak Karak
Aş Şāfī
Al Qaṭrānah
Al Jafr

ISRAEL

SAUDI
ARABIA

34° 35° 36°
33° 33°
32° 32°
31° 31°
30° 30°

The designations employed and the presentation of material on this map do not imply the expression of any opinion whatsoever on the part of the Secretariat of the United Nations concerning the legal status of any country, territory, city or area or of its authorities or concerning the delimitation of its frontiers or boundaries.

Map No. 3584 Rev. 2   UNITED NATIONS
January 2004

Department of Peacekeeping Operations
Cartographic Section

INTRODUCTION

Let me die with the Philistines. — Samson (Judges 16:30)

Could Samson, the Nazirite in the ancient land of Canaan, have been the first suicide militant? The story of Samson, which comes to us from chapters 13–16 in the book of Judges of the Bible, is intriguing, not least because his ultimate act of sacrifice took place in what is today Gaza, a place that has produced many suicide bombers since the early 1990s. Captured by the powerful Philistines, who oppressed the Israelites, Samson was tortured, blinded, and forced to toil in prison. One day he was beckoned to entertain the leaders of the Philistines in their temple, where they were to offer a sacrifice unto their god, Dagon. Unable to see, Samson asked a servant that he be moved to the pillars of the temple so that he could lean on them for rest. In an act of faith and vengeance, he summoned all his strength to bring down the two central pillars holding up the temple, killing himself and his tormentors, "so the dead which he slew at his death were more than they which he slew in his life."

The tale of Samson and the Philistines shows us that the allure of martyrdom is not a recent development. Throughout history one finds the willingness to die for a cause or higher purpose. Early Christian martyrs willingly endured some of the most gruesome tortures humankind has been able to muster, rather than renounce their faith to please the powers that be. We have seen similar determination to die in Islamic history: in the early battles of the Prophet Muhammad against the unbelievers of Mecca; in the fight waged by eleventh-century Persia's Shia sect, known as the Ismalis-Nizari, or, more commonly, *hashishiyun* (assassins); and in the struggles of Muslim communities in southwestern India, Aceh in modern-day Indonesia, and Mindanao in southern Philippines against Western colonial rule in the eighteenth and nineteenth centuries.[1]

One may object that the story of Samson is inappropriate in a discussion of suicide bombers because he hardly qualifies as a suicide terrorist. After all, he killed those in power, who had tortured him and would probably have killed him, and he did not target ordinary civilians, women, and children. A faithful "martyr" fighting oppression would be a better depiction.

But how one describes acts of self-immolation committed in order to kill others is a task fraught with controversy. Those who support these acts of violence prefer to call them "martyrdom operations," and their perpetrators "heroes" and "freedom fighters." Those who oppose them prefer to call them "homicide bombers," "suicide terrorists," or "suicidal murderers."

These are highly charged, normative terms that do not aid in the effort to analyze and explain this deadly phenomenon. Therefore, in this book I choose the more descriptive and commonly used term "suicide bomber," or "human bomb," which I define as *an individual who willingly uses his or her body to carry or deliver explosives or explosive materials to attack, kill, or maim others.* These attacks usually target civilians, but they can be used alongside conventional battlefield attacks against soldiers, as witnessed in some operations by the Liberation Tigers of Tamil Eelam (LTTE) in Sri Lanka and, more recently, insurgents in Iraq and Israel. Key to this definition is the requirement of self-immolation in order to execute an operation—the death of the bomber is a necessary part of carrying out an attack. This is different from a high-risk operation, wherein the death of the attacker is likely but not necessary to the execution of an attack. Moreover, suicide bombings are different from operations in which the attackers fight until the end in the hope of achieving martyrdom. In the latter, while the intent is still to die, the death of the individual is not necessary for the operation to take place. These distinctions may seem overly academic, but it is necessary to have a strict conceptual definition of this phenomenon in order both to collect precise and comparable data across the universe of cases and to analyze its underlying causes.

The introduction of suicide bombings in the modern world, as defined in this report, is most commonly associated with the Japanese kamikaze pilots of World War II.[2] At Okinawa alone, in 1945, more than one thousand suicide pilots were used to kill nearly five thousand American service personnel.[3] The widespread use of suicide operations reemerged during the 1980s. In Iran, tens of thousands of young boys volunteered for the Bassidj organization, which promoted self-sacrifice to defend the revolution from the invading Iraqi army. Young men rushed headlong into minefields, using their bodies to clear the way for the advancing Iranian forces. In Lebanon, Shia militants in Islamic Jihad organized the suicide bombings of the U.S. embassy and U.S. and French barracks in Beirut during 1983.[4]

From 1983 to 1986 there were 29 additional suicide missions in the Middle East, most of which were carried out in 1985 (22 attacks) by secular pro-Syrian groups. This form of violence continued into the 1990s, mainly by Hezbollah against Israeli targets in southern Lebanon.[5]

Outside the Middle East, suicide bombers emerged in Sri Lanka. The "Black Tigers" of the Tamil Tigers have led the pack in the number and sophistication of suicide missions, which succeeded in killing a defense minister in March 1991, chief of naval staff in November 1992, former prime minister of India in May 1991, and president of Sri Lanka in May 1993.[6] According to one estimate, since July 5, 1987, the date of its first suicide operation, the LTTE has carried out at least 250 such attacks. Unlike the groups that preceded them, the Tamil Tigers have no moral qualms about using children and women in their operations.[7]

Suicide terrorism was also deployed by the Marxist Kurdistan Workers Party (PKK) in Turkey and by ethnonationalist and Islamist Chechens in Russia. In both instances, women bombers played a major role in these attacks. Perhaps the most intense deployment of suicide bombers has occurred in Iraq since the toppling of Saddam Hussein in 2003. Hardly a day passes without news of one or more suicide attacks. These attacks have targeted American soldiers, United Nations and humanitarian centers, Iraqi police recruitment centers, Shia mosques, Kurdish politicians, and ordinary civilians at election booths. In at least one instance, insurgents sent as many as nine suicide bombers in one day.

Since the 1980s we have seen suicidal attacks in Afghanistan, Egypt, India, Indonesia, Iran, Iraq, Israel, Kenya, Kuwait, Lebanon, Morocco, Pakistan, Palestinian territories, Russia, Saudi Arabia, Sri Lanka, Tunisia, Turkey, the United Kingdom, the United States, and Yemen.[8] Indeed, since the 1980s, while the phenomenon of international terrorism has seen a general decline, suicide terrorism's share of the total attacks has been on the rise, resulting in more casualties per terrorist attack than in previous decades.[9] Suicide bombings are an increasingly accepted mode of violence among some groups in Muslim societies, particularly in the Palestinian territories, Chechnya, and, more recently, Iraq, Pakistan, and Saudi Arabia.

The widespread use of suicide attacks suggests that terrorism has become more lethal in its intent and now constitutes a major threat to national and international security. The specter of an attack combining suicide bombing with weapons of mass destruction concerns many intelligence analysts in Europe and the United States.[10] The attacks of September 11, 2001, in the United States have resulted in two wars, a coordinated international effort to fight terrorism abroad, and domestic legislation that curtailed civil liberties at home. Suicide attacks in Russia have resulted, at least in part, in a rollback of democratic reforms as President Vladimir Putin consolidated power in his office, presumably to strengthen his ability to fight terrorism. Suicide bombers in Israel have killed and injured hundreds of people and effectively derailed the peace process between Palestinians and Israelis, and could derail the entire ongoing effort to solidify a fragile truce between Palestinians and Israelis.[11]

This book sheds light on the campaign of suicide attacks that took place in the second Palestinian uprising, known as the al-Aqsa Intifada, which began in September 2000. Research on Palestinian suicide bombers shows that the phenomenon is a complex one that cannot be explained by a single overarching motivation. To understand this form of extreme violence, we must tackle the problem at three levels of analysis: individual motivations, organizational imperatives, and societal conflicts. At each level of analysis different variables explain why individuals, organizations, and societies embrace suicidal violence.

At the level of the individual, as the Palestinian case study shows, appeals rooted in religious redemption, national salvation, and community ties create psychological and cultural inducements to take the leap toward a "heroic" end. Organizations may be able to manipulate some individuals to carry out suicide attacks, but when suicidal violence reaches such high levels as those witnessed in the Palestinian, Chechen, and Iraqi insurgencies, we must go beyond simple notions of "brainwashing" or religious indoctrination and explore how militant groups can persuasively frame acts of self-sacrifice as legitimate and necessary means to achieving liberation. Suicide bombers are not significantly different from other rebels or soldiers around the world who are willing to engage in high-risk activism out of a sense of duty and obligation to their families, comrades, communities, and God. The leap from high-risk activism to self-sacrificing violence is not a gigantic one. Militant groups frame suicide attacks as acts of unparalleled heroism, as means to religious and national salvation, and as opportunities for empowerment and vengeance, and in doing so they foster the myth of the "heroic martyr," which inspires future volunteers for suicide attacks.

At the level of organizations, the Palestinian case suggests, strategic calculation in asymmetric warfare is the primary motivation for deploying human bombs. While many individual bombers find in religion, nationalism, or community the inspiration to carry out a suicide attack, organizational leaders are primarily motivated by the tactical advantages of suicide bombings.[12] Asymmetry in power compels the weak to innovate in order to surprise opponents and circumvent their stronger capabilities. Human bombs are smart bombs that are versatile, accurate, and extremely lethal. They are also relatively inexpensive, and their psychological impact on the enemy is potent. In some instances, the use of suicide bombings is intended to muster organizational support in the face of factional competition among insurgent groups. In such cases, the intended effect of suicide bombings is not liberation per se, but organizational maintenance or survival. Whichever the case, religious and nationalist appeals are merely instruments of organizational imperatives. The culture of martyrdom is intended not for its own sake but for the purpose of generating volunteers to fulfill organizational strategies.

At the level of society, as the Palestinian case shows, societal support for suicidal violence stems from a convergence of polarizing conflicts and legitimizing authority. Extreme violence can be facilitated by groups or communities feeling overwhelming threats by external enemies in the course of political conflict. In Palestine, intense feelings of victimization underpin societal support for suicide bombings. In the opening two months of the al-Aqsa uprising, before the sustained deployment of suicide attacks by Palestinian factions, the tactics employed by the Israeli occupying authorities to quell Palestinian rioting and shootings served to polarize the conflict rather than contain the violence. Confronted with what they saw as excessive use of force, Palestinians began calling for just retribution against Israelis. When militant factions such as Hamas and Islamic Jihad dispatched human bombs, the Palestinian communities in the occupied territories felt empowered in the face of Israel's superior military capabilities. Suicide bombings created an existential crisis for Israel and forced it to respond with harsher measures, resulting in a security dilemma in which actions by one party to enhance its security deepened feelings of insecurity on the other side.

The violence, however, was not driven solely by the security dilemma—legitimizing authorities promoted or acquiesced to extreme violence. Suicide bombers and their organizers can be constrained by religious and political authorities that choose to resist the culture of martyrdom and exercise repressive measures to halt suicide attacks. The failure of these authorities to take measures that raise doubts about the legitimacy of suicide bombings is important for this phenomenon to grow. In this case, the Palestinian Authority, headed by Yasser Arafat, failed to unequivocally denounce the bombings and indeed promoted a culture of martyrdom through its media. Religious authorities inside Palestine and in the larger Muslim world also failed to condemn attacks against civilians but instead conferred the status of "martyrs" on Palestinian human bombs. In doing so, they fed the culture of martyrdom and gave legitimacy to recruiters of suicide bombers.

These findings tell us that the study of suicide bombers cannot be reduced to individual motivations, organizational strategies, or societal contexts. The case of Palestinian suicide bombers in the uprising illustrates the complex nature of suicide terrorism. Although the findings of this book are derived from a thorough study of the Palestinian case, the three-level analytical framework is instructive for studying suicide terrorism and extreme political violence in other contexts, such as Iraq and Chechnya. It may well be that one cannot develop a complete and convincing explanation of suicide terrorism without investigating why individuals, organizations, and societies embrace martyrdom.

1

EXPLANATIONS OF
SUICIDE TERRORISM

S uicide bombings evoke shock and incredulity: How can human beings strap explosives around their bodies, walk into crowded public spaces, and blow themselves up with the intent of killing men, women, and children? Why do organizations adopt suicidal violence as a tactic in their struggle against opponents? Why do some societies venerate "martyrdom operations" and accept their perpetrators as heroes? How can we explain this rapidly growing phenomenon?

There are several explanations of suicide bombings, ranging from religious fanaticism and psychological trauma to group dynamics and strategic calculation. Each of these perspectives contains valuable insights, but each has its shortcomings, too. This chapter offers a brief review and critique of the prevailing explanations of suicide bombers.

RELIGIOUS FANATICISM

Religious fanaticism is one of the most common explanations for why individuals volunteer to become human bombs. At its core, this argument maintains that charismatic religious figures such as Osama Bin Laden and Ayatollah Khomeini sanction suicide attacks and promise their volunteers eternal salvation in heaven, where they will reap many rewards. These seemingly authoritative religious personalities selectively highlight texts and traditions that demand violent struggles against real and perceived enemies. In doing so, they frame suicide attacks as a fulfillment of God's imperative and as a vehicle for salvation and paradise.[1]

Proponents of this perspective point out that many of the recent bombers—those in Israel, Iraq, Chechnya, Pakistan, and Afghanistan, and al Qaeda terrorists in Europe and the United States—are religious fundamentalists with deep faith and Manichaean worldviews. Indeed, many justify their attacks by reference to Qur'anic passages and traditions that call for jihad and martyrdom in the path of God. As we shall see in the Palestinian case, many of the bombers appear to fall into this category.[2]

9

But despite its intuitive appeal, this explanation is not entirely convincing. First, it does not explain why many nonreligious individuals become suicide bombers, as in the case of the Sri Lankan Tamil Tigers. These are not fundamentalists and do not justify their suicide attacks in religious terms. Yet from 1987 to 2000 they carried out an effective campaign of suicide attacks that exceeded in number religious suicide bombings. Secular suicide terrorists can also be found in the PKK, fighting for independence from Turkey; the al-Aqsa Martyrs Brigades and the Popular Front for the Liberation of Palestine, fighting against Israel; and the Japanese kamikazes of World War II. Second, this theory does not explain why radical religious authorities gain a following in the first place. Given that notions of jihad and martyrdom are contested concepts subject to competing interpretations, why have radical appeals gained privileged legitimacy over more moderate ones? Is the charisma of fanatical leaders sufficient to convince young people to make the ultimate sacrifice, or must there be additional factors such as societal conflicts or cultural facilitators that push individuals to give up their lives? Is the success of the religious fanatics strictly bound up with their persuasive capacity, or is the political environment a crucial determinant of the credibility of their appeals? Finally, given that notions of jihad and martyrdom have existed since the early days of Islam, why has martyrdom been only an intermittent feature of Islamic history, and why have suicide bombings become prevalent only in the last two decades of the twentieth century and the opening decade of the twenty-first?

There can be little doubt that religious appeals play an important part in inspiring many people to become suicide bombers, but the causal link between religious inspiration and suicide attacks is not a direct one. One must situate these appeals in broader societal conflicts that allow radical ideologies to resonate with the wider public.

PSYCHOLOGICAL TRAUMA

A number of writers claim that psychological trauma is at the root of volunteerism for suicide attacks. In societies befallen by violent conflicts, personal trauma and bereavement create psychic pain that demands a psychological response. Images of lost friends or family, experiences of humiliation, and the overwhelming weight of daily risks associated with living under violent conditions result in such feelings as survivor's guilt, emotional suffering, and a sense of a foreshortened future.[3] All these psychological feelings lead some to seek an outlet in violence toward real and perceived enemies. Radical ideologies appeal to these individuals seeking vengeance against those who have inflicted pain on them and on their families and communities. For example, the Palestinian psychologist Eyad El-Sarraj attributes suicide bombings to a generation of Palestinian youth who grew up under the first Palestinian uprising and saw their parents and loved ones humiliated by Israeli soldiers.[4] The appeal of suicide bombings is that it offers victims of psychological trauma a heroic way out of their misery and powerlessness.

It is difficult to critique this position without a background in psychology. However, a few criticisms come immediately to mind. First, trauma and emotional distress can manifest in violent means other than suicide bombings, so the choice to become a human bomb is not explained by psychological mechanisms alone. We must ask, why have these traumatized individuals turned into suicide attackers as opposed to conventional terrorists that place bombs in crowded places and walk away? Second, given the trauma of the first Palestinian uprising and other conflicts around the world, why have we not seen more suicide bombings during those times or in those places? Trauma and bereavement abound in the world, but suicide bombings are not as widespread as we might expect, despite the rising trend of suicide attacks in the Muslim world. Third, given that individuals rely on organizations for supplying explosives, training, and intelligence on targets, how can this approach explain organizational decisions to adopt suicide bombings? Are organizations also acting out of a feeling of trauma, or are they motivated by other factors, such as strategy or factional competition?

These criticisms do not negate the value of the psychological approach; they merely point out that psychological factors are not sufficient to explain why individuals and organizations become suicide bombers. In the case of the Palestinians, bereavement appears to have played a role in promoting suicide attacks, but not always in the narrow sense of individuals seeking vengeance for their loved ones. Instead, ordinary individuals are moved by focal events that highlight the threat posed to their communities and nation. Such events are framed by militant groups as opportunities to avenge the community and redeem the nation.

GROUP DYNAMICS

A number of researchers assert that group dynamics are the key to understanding suicide bombings. The bonds of camaraderie developed in underground networks cause individuals to submerge their individual identities into a group identity.[5] As a result, when a group embarks on the path of violent militancy, those individuals who are inclined to back out feel an overwhelming sense of commitment to the group. Backing out is seen as a betrayal of one's brothers, or an act of cowardly retreat when others are willing to step up to the task.[6] Group dynamics work in other ways, too. Family and friendship ties lead survivors in a violent conflict to feel the urge to honor those they have lost by avenging their deaths. The causal mechanism is not necessarily that of psychological trauma; instead, the bond of friendship and commitment to a group leads individuals to continue the struggle so that those who died before them did not do so in vain.

As with the psychological trauma approach, it is difficult to fully critique this perspective without a thorough training in psychology and the sociology of groups. However, as with the psychological trauma approach, some of the shortcomings of this explanation are apparent. First, group dynamics do not explain why groups adopt suicide bombings rather than conventional methods of insurgency. The choice of method cannot be explained by group psychology. Second, as research will show, in many instances suicide bombers were recruited from outside terrorist organizations for a variety of reasons. Moreover, many volunteers seek out organizations rather than the reverse, and in a few cases, individuals shifted from one organization to another in order to expedite their suicide mission. Third, if group dynamics are sufficient to sustain a campaign of suicide attacks, why do militant organizations expend resources and energy to promote a culture of martyrdom in society, engaging in rituals, ceremonies, and public propaganda to legitimize suicide bombers? Does this suggest that societal factors are important for the recruitment of suicide bombers?

STRATEGIC CALCULATION

The study of political violence has long been influenced by rationalist explanations, which maintain that despite its fanatical aura, suicide terrorism is actually a rational and purposeful method of political contention in the context of asymmetrical power. They point out that human bombs conduct their missions with greater versatility and accuracy and are less likely to be captured and forced to inform on their recruiters. They are "smart bombs" that can make operational adjustments during an attack to increase the kill rate. Also, suicide bombings save the organization from having to lose many valuable members in a single attack.[7]

Acts of terrorism, generally speaking, attempt to influence three audiences: the society being attacked, the constituency represented by the terrorists, and international public opinion. Suicide terrorism achieves these three tasks with great efficiency and effectiveness. Its psychological impact on the target audience is much more potent than that of conventional means because it highlights the determination of the insurgents and sends the message that "we are not deterred by death."[8] Professor Robert Pape at the University of Chicago sees suicide violence as particularly effective against democracies, which may be sensitive to high casualty rates. Terrorists may calculate that a wave of suicide attacks will raise the costs for the affected populace and force it to push its government to shift policies in order to end the violence. Islamic Jihad's attacks on American and French personnel in Lebanon in 1983, which subsequently resulted in the withdrawal of multinational forces from the region, are a classic example of how this tactic could work.[9]

When it comes to one's constituency, suicide attacks signal that there are determined individuals willing to sacrifice for the nation, so one should not let their sacrifice go in vain. In other words, suicide attacks serve as a wake-up call to others, asking them to make similar sacrifices for the cause.[10] The attacks could also be intended to increase the popularity of the organizations carrying them out. Groups seeking to satisfy their constituency and maintain their market share of public support will employ this tactic repeatedly to outbid competitors.[11] As for international public opinion, suicide attacks capture headlines and make people wonder, "What's going on?" In these instances, suicide attacks can be a double-edged sword: On the one hand, they may raise sympathy for the victims of attacks, but on the other, they make observers question the conditions that are leading people to kill themselves in acts of desperation.

The "rational actor" approach offers a counterintuitive solution to the puzzle of suicidal terror, but it also prompts a number of critical inquiries. First, do the communiqués of suicide bombers validate that the bombers adopt a strictly strategic or tactical rationale in their selection of tactics? Can we reconcile the self-image of the suicidal terrorist with the instrumental calculation of his or her recruiters? In the case of Palestinian suicide bombers, a careful reading of their statements suggests multiple motivations that are invariably infused with religious and nationalist inspirations, not strategic or tactical considerations. Second, if the strategic logic of suicide bombings is abundantly obvious, why do militant organizations exert a great deal of time, effort, and resources to honor and venerate the "heroic" deeds of their martyrs? In other words, why do radical groups seek to promote a culture of martyrdom if instrumental reasoning is sufficient to convince the broader public of the utility of suicide bombings?

Third, how can the strategic approach explain the decision of individuals to accept the role of martyr, especially when these individuals will not live to enjoy the fruits of their struggle? Rationalist explanations are based on the belief that individuals calculate costs and benefits before taking risks. This cannot be the case with suicide bombers, who bear all the costs and enjoy none of the benefits, because they are dead. Some may argue that the rewards of the afterlife promised by religion serve as the prerequisite benefits for making the decision to self-immolate.[12] This rationality is problematic, however, because both the ends (rewards in the afterlife) and means (martyrdom in the path of God) are contingent on the bomber's deep religious faith. The rationalizing of self-sacrifice is possible because of a transcendent belief system that links death with heavenly rewards, not just with the instrumentality of human reasoning. If this is the case, the wall separating religious fanaticism and strategic rationality withers away.

Others explain individual motivations to engage in suicide bombings, arguing that community honor and respect for "martyrs" and their families factor into the cost-benefit calculations of suicide bombers. There are two problems with this line of reasoning. First, it does not seem logical for individuals to seek rewards that they cannot partake in, because the rewards are dependent on their self-immolation; dead bombers cannot enjoy greater community respect bestowed on them following an attack. Second, even if "honor" rewards for surviving family members can inspire self-sacrifice, then we must explore the cultural norms that hold martyrdom as an honorable act deserving of respect in the first place. In this instance, there is no escaping the role of culture as a determinant of what constitutes rewards in human calculations.

The preceding analysis suggests that rationalist approaches can explain organizational decisions to employ suicide bombings, but they cannot explain why individuals accept the role of "martyr" in fulfilling organizational objectives. The following chapters present an analytical framework based on three levels of analysis: organizational strategies, individual motivations, and societal conflicts. Some of the aforementioned theories are incorporated into this framework to offer a comprehensive explanation of suicide bombings.

2

PALESTINIAN SUICIDE BOMBINGS
SINCE 1993

An in-depth case study of the Palestinian suicide bombers during the second Palestinian uprising of September 2000–February 2005 can help us explore the underlying causes and dynamics of suicide terrorism.[1] Suicide bombings did not begin during the al-Aqsa Intifada. As early as September 1993 Hamas and Islamic Jihad organized suicide attacks, principally against Israeli civilians inside Israel (see chart 1). From 1993 to 2000 these two groups deployed some 33 bombers in 26 separate attacks, producing 159 deaths and 927 injuries.

Chart 1: Palestinian Suicide Bombings, September 1993–February 2005

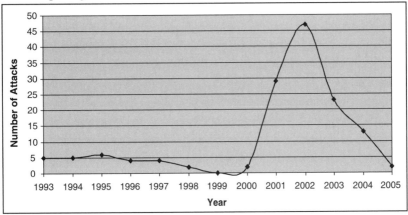

As early as the mid-1980s, Fathi al-Shiqaqi, one of the founding leaders of the Palestinian Islamic Jihad (assassinated in 1995), advocated the use of "martyrdom operations" to counterbalance Israel's superior military capabilities. Suicide attacks in Lebanon by Hezbollah and other nationalist factions against Israel and Western multinational forces during the 1980s demonstrated the effectiveness of this tactic. However, the organizational nexus between Hamas and Islamic Jihad, on the one hand, and Hezbollah

17

in Lebanon, on the other, took place in 1992–93. On December 17, 1992, Israel, under Prime Minister Yitzhak Rabin, deported 415 Islamic activists from the West Bank and Gaza into southern Lebanon following the killing of five Israeli servicemen. For much of 1993, these activists were forced to live in makeshift camps on the desolate hillsides of southern Lebanon. The Lebanese government refused to take them in, and Israel refused to let them back. As a result, Hezbollah provided them material and moral support. In the process, many of these activists and leaders held discussions with Hezbollah regarding strategies and tactics for resistance.

After the signing of the Declaration of Principles in September 1993 between the Palestine Liberation Organization (PLO) and Israel, most of those expelled returned to the territories with a determination to oppose the peace process. Hamas and Islamic Jihad faced a dilemma, however. On the one hand, the Oslo accords threatened to marginalize the two groups (Hamas in particular) politically after they achieved national prominence during the first Palestinian uprising, in 1987–93. They did not want to join the Palestinian Authority (PA), because such a move necessitated recognition of Israel and the two-state solution, which is anathema to their Islamist outlook. Hamas and Islamic Jihad view Palestine as an Islamic endowment (*waqf*) that cannot be divided or negotiated away. On the other hand, Hamas and Islamic Jihad could not simply engage in suicide bombings against Israel without risking repression from the PA, which, under the Oslo accords, was obliged to fight anti-Israeli terrorism stemming from areas under Palestinian control. Indeed, the PA exercised its repressive powers against militant groups in 1994, 1995, and 1996 following suicide attacks that threatened to derail the peace process.

To circumvent these political limitations, Hamas and Islamic Jihad linked their suicide attacks against Israelis to specific "provocative" actions taken by Israel. Such an action came in February 1994, when Baruch Goldstein, a Jewish settler from New York living in the settlement of Kiryat Arba, massacred 29 Muslim worshippers praying in the Tomb of the Patriarchs, or Ibrahimi Mosque, in Hebron. Hamas avenged these killings by sending two suicide bombers in April of that year, killing 13 people and injuring over 70. A similar provocation occurred in January 1996, when Israeli intelligence assassinated Yahya Ayyash, famously known as "the Engineer." Ayyash, the chief bomb maker for Hamas, was responsible for a number of suicide bombings. The daring assassination, using a bomb hidden in a mobile phone and involving a betrayal by close aides, was a shock to Hamas. Following the assassination, Hamas unleashed 4 suicide attacks, killing 57 Israelis and injuring over 130.

Given these opportunities, Hamas and Islamic Jihad sought to derail the peace process while claiming they were merely responding to Israeli transgressions. The PA found it difficult to take drastic measures against the groups when they appeared to be defending the Palestinian people. As a result, limited violence by radicals during the peace process satisfied Hamas's and Islamic Jihad's core constituencies without forcing the groups to enter into a civil war with the PA.

The contained violence of the peace years broke loose during the al-Aqsa uprising. Suicide bombings emerged as one of the preferred tactics of Palestinian militants. Both religious and secular factions repeatedly conducted "martyrdom operations" in their latest insurgency against Israel and have convinced the wider Palestinian public of their legitimacy, leading some to argue that a culture of martyrdom has penetrated this conflicted society.[2] During the Oslo peace process years (1993–2000), most Palestinians rejected suicidal attacks against Israeli civilians. However, during the al-Aqsa Intifada, the overwhelming majority supported such attacks, despite fluctuating levels of support. For instance, in a March 1996 poll conducted by the Palestinian Center for Policy and Survey Research, only 21.1 percent of Palestinians in the West Bank and Gaza expressed support for suicide bombings. The highest support for suicide bombings during the peace process years never exceeded 32.7 percent, which was in September 1997, when Benjamin Netanyahu, the hawkish Likud leader, was in office. In contrast, an October 2003 poll by the same research center found that 74.5 percent of Palestinians supported suicide bombings (see chart 2). Only in March 2005, after the Palestinians and Israelis agreed on a mutual cease-fire, did support for suicide bombings dip substantially: 29.1 percent continued to support them, while 67.1 percent opposed them.[3]

Suicide bombings since 2000 have taken on a new character, both quantitatively and qualitatively. From September 1993 to September 2000, there averaged fewer than 4 bombings a year. In the latest cycle of violence, however, suicide bombings have been carried out monthly, weekly, and sometimes daily. From October 2000 to February 2005 there were

Chart 2: Palestinian Support for Suicide Bombings in Public Opinion Data, 1996–2004

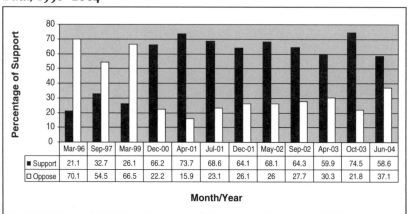

	Mar-96	Sep-97	Mar-99	Dec-00	Apr-01	Jul-01	Dec-01	May-02	Sep-02	Apr-03	Oct-03	Jun-04
■ Support	21.1	32.7	26.1	66.2	73.7	68.6	64.1	68.1	64.3	59.9	74.5	58.6
□ Oppose	70.1	54.5	66.5	22.2	15.9	23.1	26.1	26	27.7	30.3	21.8	37.1

Month/Year

approximately 116 suicide attacks—an average of more than 27 attacks per year—carried out by 127 bombers (see chart 1). Many more attacks were foiled by Israeli forces. (For a list of the names of suicide bombers since 1993, the dates of their attacks, their targets, and other information, see appendix A.)

Suicide bombings since 2000 have changed in qualitative ways. Before then, suicide bombings were the domain of Islamic militants belonging to Hamas and Islamic Jihad. But since 2000 this mode of violence has been adopted by secular factions such as the semi-Marxist Popular Front for the Liberation of Palestine (PFLP) and a Fatah faction known as the al-Aqsa Martyrs Brigades (AMB) (see chart 3 on p. 22). Moreover, whereas previously men were the only ones to conduct suicide bombings, in recent years women have taken up the explosive belt.[4] Finally, whereas previously suicide bombings involved a relatively long cycle of recruitment, indoctrination, and training, in recent times they have been carried out by volunteers with no more than a few days or weeks of preparation.[5]

How are human bombs recruited? Hamas and Islamic Jihad allocate the tasks required for carrying out suicide bombings among at least three cells, possibly four. One cell is responsible for gathering intelligence on a target and determining the best way to deliver the bomber to the target. According to Salah Shahada, the general commander of Hamas's military wing (assassinated in 2002), field operatives videotape the target and submit it along with a report to a military committee to approve the operation. Another cell is responsible for recruiting and mentally preparing the bomber for the attack. A third cell is responsible for preparing the explosives and delivering the bomber to the target. Hamas and Islamic Jihad generally speaking, have five criteria for selecting potential suicide bombers: (1) They must be pious Muslims; (2) they must be able to pass as Israelis, especially if the operation is to take place inside Israel; (3) they must be mature, usually over the age of eighteen and usually unmarried; (4) they must not stand out in any significant way that raises suspicion at major security checkpoints, such as being wanted for prior activism, and must demonstrate that they can be discreet in the company of family and friends before an operation; and (5) they must not be without siblings or be the main breadwinners in their families.[6] It is not entirely clear what criteria the AMB or the PFLP adopt in selecting suicide bombers.[7]

Sometimes recruiters seek out potential bombers in religious study groups known as *usras* (literally, "family"). Once a person is identified as a potential bomber, his or her recruitment takes place outside the study group.[8] Sometimes operatives monitor local mosques for pious young men and observe their attendance and behavior over a period of time before recruiters befriend them. In the al-Aqsa uprising, volunteerism for suicide attacks increased significantly; many organizations declare proudly that there are more volunteers than there are explosive belts. In the case of volunteers, being connected to a network of militants or to extended family members with ties to military wings of radical groups is the main way to reach recruiters. Invariably, recruiters inquire about an individual's history, including his or her personal habits, political inclinations, and emotional composure. Usually there is a gestation period in which the recruit is observed from a distance to make sure he or she is not compromised or does not fail to meet the aforementioned criteria. When the recruits are volunteers, some recruiters question their motives and try to discourage them in order to get a sense of their determination. Indoctrination and psychological preparation involves intense political and religious discussions spanning several weeks. Bombers view videos of earlier operations and discuss earlier bombers and the benefits of martyrdom in Islam.[9] According to Nasra Hassan, the recruiters focus on six chapters from the Qur'an because of their relevance to faith, jihad, and martyrdom: chapter 2, al-Baqara;

Chart 3: Successful Suicide Bombings, by Group, October 2000–December 2003

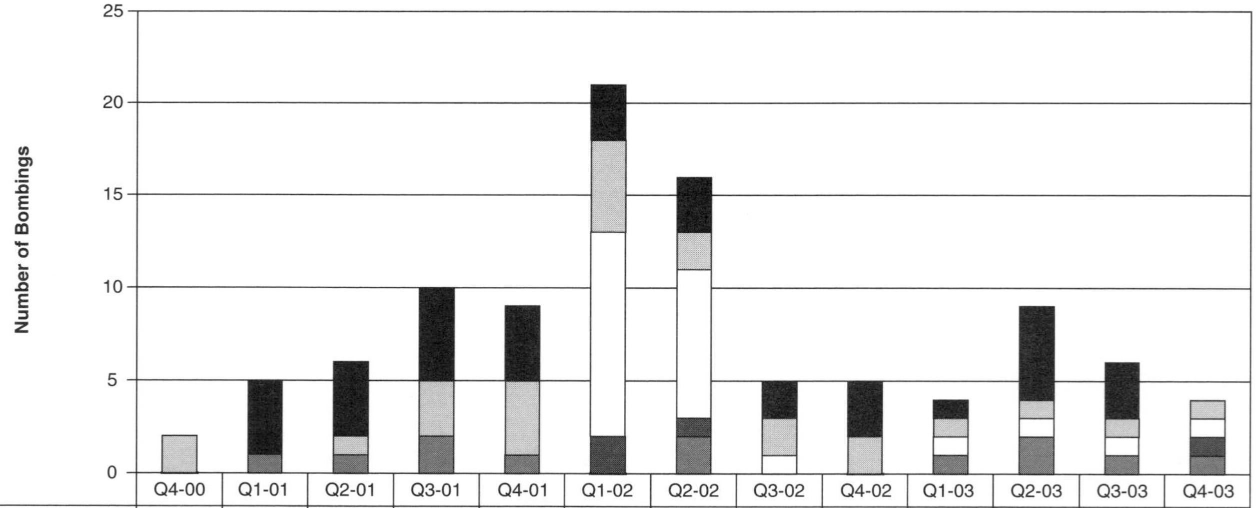

	Q4-00	Q1-01	Q2-01	Q3-01	Q4-01	Q1-02	Q2-02	Q3-02	Q4-02	Q1-03	Q2-03	Q3-03	Q4-03
Total	2	5	6	10	9	21	16	5	5	4	9	6	4
Hamas	0	4	4	5	4	3	3	2	3	1	5	3	0
Islamic Jihad	2	0	1	3	4	5	2	2	2	1	1	1	1
AMB	0	0	0	0	0	11	8	1	0	1	1	1	1
PFLP	0	0	0	0	0	2	1	0	0	0	0	0	1
Other / Joint Op.	0	1	1	2	1	0	2	0	0	1	2	1	1

Chart 4: Monthly Percentages of Palestinians and Israelis Killed/Injured in Conflict, September 2000–December 2003

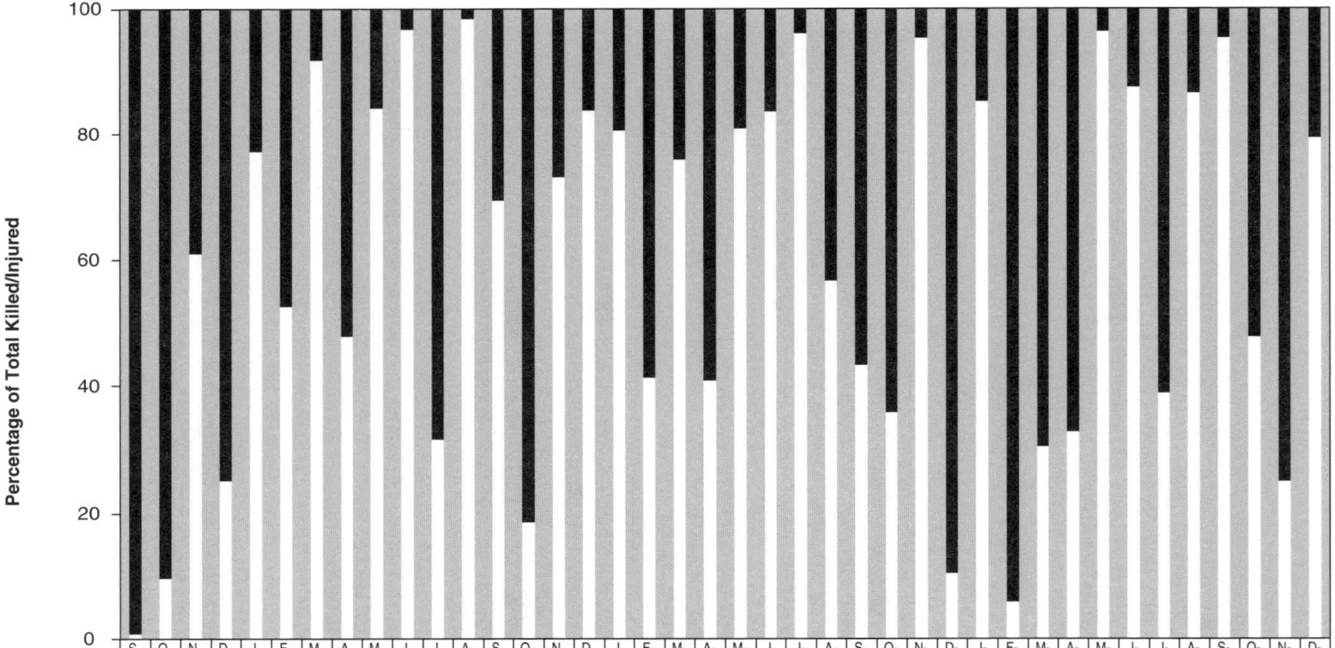

	S-00	O-00	N-00	D-00	J-01	F-01	M-01	A-01	M-01	J-01
■ Palestinians	232	207	62	89	20	36	11	75	39	5
□ Israelis	2	22	97	30	68	40	124	69	209	147

	J-01	A-01	S-01	O-01	N-01	D-01	J-02	F-02	M-02	A-02
■ Palestinians	41	3	54	35	15	101	57	146	255	254
□ Israelis	19	186	123	8	41	529	238	103	807	176

	M-02	J-02	J-02	A-02	S-02	O-02	N-02	D-02	J-03	F-03
■ Palestinians	57	47	8	55	93	143	3	215	32	113
□ Israelis	243	242	197	72	71	80	61	25	186	7

	M-03	A-03	M-03	J-03	J-03	A-03	S-03	O-03	N-03	D-03
■ Palestinians	283	178	4	17	11	26	4	104	15	7
□ Israelis	124	87	105	120	7	168	82	95	5	27

chapter 3, al-Imran; chapter 8, al-Anfal; chapter 9, al-Tawba; chapter 55, al-Rahman; and chapter 103, al-Asr. During the final stages of preparation, a few days before an operation, the "living martyr" goes into isolation along with close companions from the preparation cell to strengthen his resolve. During this period, the bomber prepares his will and testament and is videotaped declaring his intention to become a martyr. This final step is important in solidifying the commitment of the bomber—it is an act of "bridge burning" because to retreat beyond this point constitutes a failure to meet one's commitment to the cause, to God, and to the nation.[10]

Observers of the second intifada often comment that suicide bombers do not lend themselves to easy generalizations. Other than being Muslim, usually unmarried, and in their late teens or early twenties, the bombers have little in common.[11] Some come from modest or impoverished backgrounds, while others come from middle-class or even affluent families. Some bombers lack secondary education, while others are university students and graduates with degrees as varied as engineering, computer programming, journalism, and Islamic law. Some have been engaged in militancy since the first Palestinian uprising, while others are recent recruits who joined the movement explicitly for the purpose of carrying out a suicide mission.[12] The lack of a common profile of suicide bombers suggests that a single-factor explanation of this phenomenon is not possible.

So why do they do it? Suicidal violence on the scale seen in the Palestinian-Israeli conflict involves at least three actors: organizations that are willing to recruit, train, and dispatch suicide bombers; individuals who are willing to serve as human bombs; and societies that legitimize and venerate "martyrdom operations." We must probe at each level to uncover the causes of this deadly phenomenon.

3

ORGANIZATIONAL MOTIVES
The Strategic Logic of Insurgent Groups

I begin with the organizational motives because organizations are the essential nexus between societal conflicts and individual suicide bombers. Without organizations, aggrieved individuals cannot act out their violence in a sustained manner. Suicidal violence requires organizational tasks that include acquiring intelligence on potential targets, recruitment and preparation of potential bombers, engineering explosives for suicide attacks, transporting bombers to their targets, and issuing propaganda to promote organizational ideology, gain public support, and set the stage for future recruitment of militants.[1] What this tells us is that organizations that adopt suicide bombings require a sophisticated infrastructure, financial and material resources, and commitment at various levels of organizational membership and leadership. Without this organizational infrastructure and commitment, suicide attacks will be limited in scope and magnitude. It also tells us that suicidal violence is not a whimsical choice adopted by a single leader, no matter how charismatic or influential, irrespective of what other commanders and members think.

Suicide attacks are a strategic choice based on cost-benefit calculations by weak groups with limited resources seeking to wage war against formidable opponents. Under conditions of asymmetrical power, disadvantaged groups seek to protect their meager financial, material, and human resources and place a premium on secrecy and organizational maintenance. Therefore, militant groups utilize forms of indirect warfare to inflict damage on their opponents without exposing their organizations to undue loss of resources. Thus, groups that employ anticivilian violence—even seemingly fanatical, highly emotive, or wanton forms of violence such as suicide terrorism—are actually using an effective and rational method of asymmetrical warfare to achieve desired goals. Under certain circumstances, groups come to value extreme violence because of its ability to coerce opponents, publicize grievances, disrupt the status quo, question the legitimacy of the ruling order, induce compromise, show determination, sabotage negotiations, and so on.

Palestinian insurgents would stand little chance of victory if they were to take on the Israel Defense Forces (IDF) directly. The IDF is better trained and equipped and can endure material losses thanks to the resources it commands. The Palestinian factions, on the other hand, lack sophisticated weaponry and have lost many lives through conventional hit-and-run operations without inflicting harm on the IDF. Accordingly, they have switched to "softer," that is, civilian, targets—a strategy that can terrorize Israelis, weaken their economy, and drive settlers away from the occupied territories. In defending their strategy to internal critics, Hamas's and Islamic Jihad's principal justifications for suicide bombings are not religious but instrumental in nature. Put simply, suicide bombings are promoted because they are viewed as more effective than conventional methods of resistance, and the best means to achieve the strategic aims of the Palestinian people. Azet al-Rushuq, a member of Hamas's political bureau abroad, writes, "This weapon [suicide bomber] is our winning card, which turned our weakness and feebleness into strength, and created parity never before witnessed in the history of struggle with the Zionist enemy. It also gave our people the ability to respond, deter, and inflict harm on the enemy; it no longer bears the brunt of punishment alone."[2]

This notion of a "balance of terror" was further affirmed by Muhammad Nazzal, a member of Hamas's political bureau abroad, in an interview on al-Jazeera television in August 2002. He argued that military operations within the occupied territories resulted on average in one Israeli death for every twelve Palestinians killed. In contrast, operations within Israel's 1948 borders resulted in nine Israeli deaths for every Palestinian suicide bomber.[3] He went on to argue that in the first six months of the al-Aqsa Intifada, there was a ratio of 5.1 Palestinians killed for every Israeli killed. In the six months from February to August 2002, that ratio changed to 1.7 Palestinians killed for every Israeli killed. He concluded by arguing that suicide bombings were giving Palestinians—who do not have fighter planes, Apache helicopters, tanks, and so on—strategic parity. These operations, he said, create a balance of forces. The accuracy of Nazzal's overall assessment of the equalizing power of suicide bombings may be contested, but his claim that suicide bombings have narrowed the ratio of Palestinian to Israeli deaths is supported by the evidence (see chart 4 on p. 23).

In a three-part "investigative" report by Hamas, published in April 2002 in its London-based journal, *Falastin al-Muslima* (Islamic Palestine), the authors catalog the achievements of suicide bombings for the Palestinian struggle in strictly instrumental terms. In part 1 of the report we are told that in 1999 settlements grew at a rate of 12 percent; in 2000, at 8 percent; and in 2001, at 5 percent. Moreover, fewer people came to live in Israel in 2001—only 43,000 immigrated there, whereas in the previous year 60,000 came. Many Israelis are leaving the country to live in the United States, Canada, and elsewhere because of the worsening security situation, and millions have already left. Fewer Israelis use public transportation and restaurants now, and more are using medication to remain calm.[4] In part 2, the report claims that suicide bombings have contributed to a decline in tourism, resulting in many tourist workers' losing their jobs; thirty-five hotels and fifty tourist services have closed down. Unemployment has risen.[5] In part 3, the author argues that despite the low number of Israeli soldiers killed during the uprising, the psychological impact of the insurgency on the Israeli military has been tremendous. As many as 11,200 have deserted, refusing to serve in the occupied territories.[6] Many of these claims are questionable, but they reflect Hamas's instrumental reasoning behind the use of suicide bombers.

Perhaps the most-often-made claim in support of suicide bombings is their efficacy compared to the alternative strategy of negotiations. Radical factions consistently argue that negotiations have led to a dead end and that an alternative strategy is required to achieve the national aspirations of the Palestinian people. In light of Hezbollah's "victory" in southern Lebanon in mid-2000, and the failure of the Palestinian Authority (PA) to extract the necessary concessions to establish a viable Palestinian state in late 2000, violent insurgency was framed as the optimal strategy to force the Israelis to leave Palestinian lands. In a debate aired on al-Jazeera television, between Yasser Abd Rabbo, minister of media and culture, and Ramadan Abdulla Shalah, general secretary of Islamic Jihad, Abd Rabbo requests a halt to suicide bombings because "it is obvious that Sharon wants to destroy the Palestinian Authority, its institutions and infrastructure. He has used the suicide operations as a pretext to do so. He wants to take advantage of the September 11 attacks [on the United States] to paint the Palestinians with the same brush as al Qaeda's terrorism so he can avoid the formation of a

Palestinian state. Therefore, we must not fall into his trap." He goes on to argue, "We need the support of the international community so we can balance against the Israeli occupation that legitimizes itself by portraying Palestinians as terrorists. Moreover, we should not carry out operations against civilians because it gives Israelis the excuses they need—and the international legitimacy—to harm the Palestinian public and destroy its accomplishments and institutions." Abdulla Shalah responds by arguing that "years of negotiations have not achieved the basic goals and rights of the Palestinian people. History has shown, whether history with the Israelis or history of the oppressed people around the world, that resistance is the only way to achieve your objectives."[7] Shalah makes a similar point in an interview in *al-Istiqlal*, a pro–Islamic Jihad newspaper in Gaza, on October 25, 2001. He maintains that "the shameful defeat that Israel suffered in southern Lebanon [in 2000] and which caused its army to flee in terror was not made on the negotiations table but on the battlefield and through *jihad* and martyrdom. . . . If the enemy could not bear the losses of war on the border strip with Lebanon, will it be able to withstand a long war of attrition in the heart of its security perimeters and major cities?"

In another telling debate on "martyrdom operations" aired on al-Jazeera, Hani al-Masri, political analyst and signatory to a communiqué that called for an end to suicide bombings, claims that while suicide bombings have achieved certain objectives, on balance they are detrimental to the national goals of the Palestinian people. Specifically, he argues that suicide bombings militarize the uprising and give Israel an excuse to activate its superior military capabilities to crush the resistance and achieve a decisive conclusion to the struggle. Even if the Palestinians are able to kill more Israelis than before, that in itself is not reason enough to continue with this strategy, because the goal is not to kill more people but to achieve the objectives of the Palestinian people. Suicide bombings have unified the Israelis behind the most extreme and racist elements in Israeli society, al-Masri argues, thus making it difficult for the Palestinians to negotiate an equitable settlement to the conflict. Finally, he concludes, after the September 11 attacks on America, international support has turned completely against the Palestinians because of the suicide attacks against civilians.

In response to al-Masri's arguments, Muhammad Nazzal presents a series of counterarguments that are instrumental at their core. Nazzal argues that it is not the resistance that is leading to an unfavorable conclusion of the struggle, but rather the failed strategy of negotiations among unequal powers that is giving Israelis control over 80 percent of the land of historic Palestine. The resistance is preventing such a conclusion by depriving the Israelis of security, harming their economy, and disrupting their occupation. As for world opinion, Nazzal vociferously claims that "world opinion does not matter. Where is world opinion when it comes to the Jenin massacre? World opinion, especially American and European opinion, is a lie that has not served us well." As for the charge that suicide bombings kill civilians, Nazzal offers a standard reply that has come to be accepted by many Palestinians:

> In a war between two states, those who fight are combatants and those that do not are civilians. In the case of the Israeli occupation, this does not hold. It is not a struggle between two armies or two states. It is a struggle between a colonizing power with mightier forces and a modernized armory, and a helpless people with modest arms. This colonial power is nothing more than an army that possesses a state, not a state that has an army. Israeli society is overwhelmingly militarized with few genuine civilians. We define civilians as those who do not carry arms and do not fight. In the case of Israel, this applies to those who are less than 18 years old and those who are elderly; the rest are combatants. We do not kill children. We could easily go to preschools or public places where children hang out or attack the elderly, but we do not. The rest, however, whether men or women, are forcefully conscripted into the army and once a year they are recalled for at least 40 days and in cases of war or emergency.[8]

Secular groups adopted suicide terrorism, at least in part, to compete with their Islamic rivals in the factional struggle over public support. In interviews with Fatah members and those with direct access to some of Fatah's militants in the West Bank, I was told that the AMB adopted suicide bombings because the other factions seemed to be outperforming them. Many Fatah members, from whose ranks the AMB emerged, felt that Fatah initiated the uprising and Hamas was late to join it. I was repeatedly told that Hamas initially viewed the uprising as "political theater" orchestrated by the PA to achieve a final settlement with Israel. As the uprising gained momentum and Ariel Sharon came to power, Hamas joined with full force. By adopting suicide bombings, Hamas seemed to be taking the lead in liberating Palestine. One of the Fatah militants termed this development "healthy competition" in the same way that European football (soccer) teams compete with one another by constantly striving to be creative in their strategies.[9] In reality, the adoption of suicide bombings was more than mere "constructive competition"; it was about recapturing the spotlight that seemed to have been unfairly stolen by the Islamist factions.

However, the main reason the AMB adopted suicide bombings was that it felt that Israeli escalations, including the targeted assassinations of Fatah leaders, especially of Raed al-Karmi in January 2002, required a commensurate response to deter Israelis from more such attacks. When the uprising began, Fatah militias and security service employees engaged in pitched battles with Israeli forces, usually exchanging fire from afar at checkpoints. They also fired random shots at settlements adjacent to Palestinian towns in order to frighten the settlers. The intent was not necessarily to kill but to flex muscle and force settlers to flee. As the Israeli response to the uprising intensified, Fatah groups began carrying out more organized attacks, mainly shooting at settlers in bypass roads and attacking Israeli patrols. From December 2001 to January 2002, the AMB avoided suicide bombings.

Beginning in 2002, the AMB employed suicide bombers with a vengeance. They were the first to send female suicide bombers, which may have facilitated the decision of Islamic Jihad and, later, Hamas to do the same. (Hamas sent only one.) Three factors in the field of battle contributed to this shift in tactics. First, Israel's security measures made conventional attacks against soldiers nearly impossible. Closures and checkpoints, as well as improved security at bypass roads, made it very difficult to launch operations without heavy casualties. This made the option of suicide attacks appear attractive to the AMB. As one Fatah activist told me, "one says to himself, if I'm going to die, I might as well take as many of them [Israelis] with me." Second, the removal of valuable leaders, through either arrests or targeted assassinations, meant that inexperienced young leaders were less sensitive to Fatah's political needs to avoid civilian casualties and more interested in inflicting pain on the other side. In a PBS *Frontline* interview on March 26, 2002, Jihad Jaarie, a leader of the AMB in Bethlehem, explains why his group began to adopt suicide attacks against civilians:

In the beginning the National Liberation Movement [Fatah] did not use martyrdom [suicide] operations. But in our study of the enormous oppressive Israeli military might used against the Palestinian people and the Palestinian children, we had no choice but to take measures and appropriately respond to the large military operations. When the F-16 air force bombers bombard our areas and our people and families, what do the Israelis expect from us? That we answer them back with crude machine guns? Our view was that the appropriate response to such bombardment is to inflict heavy casualties on the Israeli street so that we can almost match what they inflict on us.[10]

Finally, the removal of experienced field commanders encouraged the remaining Fatah activists to cooperate in the field with the Islamist factions, initially with Islamic Jihad and later with Hamas.[11] The AMB became increasingly upset at Fatah's official line of distancing itself from AMB violence. They felt abandoned and sought support from other militant groups. This field cooperation undoubtedly consolidated the AMB's decision to deploy suicide bombers.[12]

We can summarize the instrumental reasoning of Hamas, Islamic Jihad, and the AMB with regard to suicide bombings in this way:

❖ Negotiations have failed to deliver on the legitimate rights and aspirations of the Palestinian people.

❖ Armed resistance is the best means to raise the costs of the Israeli occupation and ultimately push Israelis out of Palestinian lands.

❖ Given Israel's superior military capabilities and forces, conventional attacks inside Palestinian lands occupied in 1967 are likely to fail.

❖ Suicide bombings inside the Green Line (1949 armistice borders) are more effective in fighting the Israelis because they terrorize their populations, destroy their economy, drive away immigrants and tourists, and force the Israelis to choose between life without the occupation and death with the occupation.

❖ Israel is an armed, militarized society with a "citizen army." Therefore, it is legitimate to attack its people anywhere in historic Palestine, even if they do not don military garb.

❖ Attacking Israeli civilians is the price Israel pays for attacking Palestinian militants and civilians.

The instrumental reasoning of militant organizations suggests that strategic, not religious or cultural, considerations are the reasons why they adopted suicide bombings. However, it would be a mistake to dismiss the importance of religion, nationalism, or community in motivating individuals to carry out suicide attacks. What motivates organizations is not necessarily what motivates individuals. The communiqués of Palestinian suicide bombers clearly illustrate that the bombers do not adopt a strictly cost-benefit approach in deciding to become human bombs. A careful reading of their last wills and testaments suggests multiple motivations that are often infused with religious inspirations, desire for vengeance, and commitment to family, community, and Islam. Moreover, militant organizations exert a great deal of time, effort, and resources to honor, venerate, and celebrate the "heroic" deeds of their martyrs. They seek to promote a culture of martyrdom based on religious appeals and innovative rituals to convince the broader public of the value of suicide bombings. To probe the motivations of individual bombers, we need to look beyond strategic calculations and into the realm of religious frameworks, nationalist appeals, and community ties.

4
INDIVIDUAL MOTIVES
The Redemptive Logic of Suicide Bombers

R esearch on political violence and social movements shows that organizers of violence must draw on religion, culture, or identity to give meaning to extreme violence.[1] Religion, culture, and identity serve as "tool kits" from which organizers of collective action strategically select narratives, traditions, symbols, rituals, or repertoires of action to imbue risky activism with morality. Moreover, militant groups must align their rhetoric and ideological appeals with cultural norms and expectations, lest they fail to resonate with their target recruits.[2] Finally, the use of cultural or religious appeals to motivate collective action always involves a degree of innovation whereby old ideas are presented in new ways that appear to be simultaneously authentic and relevant for contemporary times. As Sidney Tarrow eloquently put it, "symbols of revolt are not drawn like musty costumes from a cultural closet and arrayed before the public. Nor are new meanings unrolled out of whole cloth. The costumes of revolt are woven from a blend of inherited and invented fibers into collective action frames in confrontation with opponents and elites."[3]

In the Palestinian territories, militant groups deploying suicide bombings foster a culture of martyrdom in order to generate volunteers for suicide missions. Simple notions of brainwashing and manipulated individuals must be abandoned in this case. Militant organizations have succeeded in framing self-immolation as a meaningful act of redemption. Redemption has two meanings in this context. In one sense, redemption is adherence to one's avowed identity in times when loyalty to this identity is brought into question. In this respect, redemption is about keeping a commitment to one's values and fulfilling the promises implied by those values. Rather than shy away from the challenge, individuals choose to redeem their identity through acts of heroism and sacrifice. For example, soldiers in intense combat situations, or firefighters in emergency conditions, often explain their extraordinary courage in terms of doing their job because that is who they are and what they are trained to do. In another sense, redemption is about salvation of the self or valued others from perceived dangers or errors. From a religious point of view, redemption is about saving oneself or loved ones from grave sin that could result in eternal damnation. From the point of view of nationalism, redemption is about taking extraordinary measures to save one's country from existential threats. Militant groups often call on people to engage in violence to fulfill their duty to their own values, family, friends, community, or religion. Failure to act, consequently, creates dissonance because it is perceived as a betrayal of one's ideals, loved ones, country, God, or sense of manhood.

In the Palestinian territories, militant organizations draw on three cultural and political contexts to equate suicide attacks with opportunities for redemption: religious revivalism, nationalist conflict, and community ties. Religious revivalism allows religious appeals that equate self-sacrifice with the imperative of martyrdom in the path of God to resonate in society. Nationalist conflict allows militant groups to argue that extraordinary acts of heroism are necessary for national salvation. Community ties create bonds of friendship and family loyalty that motivate individuals to seek vengeance when loved ones are killed, traumatized, or humiliated by external enemies. The statements of bombers and their organizers often weave these three elements together, so it is difficult to segregate individual motivations into a clear hierarchy of motives. Moreover, it is difficult to determine whether these elements are sufficient to motivate suicide bombings or are mere subconscious discursive ploys by which to give acts of sacrifice meaning after one has already made the decision to kill oneself. Insights from psychology and other disciplines are needed to specify the causal weight of these apparent motivations in suicide bombings. Whatever the case, there can be no doubt that religion, nationalism, and community ties have played important roles in engendering a culture of martyrdom that underpins the campaign of suicide bombings against Israel.

RELIGIOUS REDEMPTION

One cannot understand the prevailing acceptance of suicidal violence in Palestinian society—and in the Muslim world in general—without comprehending the cultural shift that has characterized Muslim societies since the 1970s. After decades of Western secularization, the Muslim world has witnessed an Islamic revival characterized by the spread of public displays of piety, growing mosque attendance, and the spread of Islamic networks, social movements, and political parties.

Beginning in the 1970s, young men and women in the universities gravitated toward Islamic social clubs and unions, and Islamic activists reaped the benefits by expanding their representation in local student elections. Where and when allowed, Islamists organized political parties and played an active role in Islamizing their politics. Networks of charity and nongovernmental mosques were created by Islamic activists who saw an opportunity to present viable public spaces free from the "corrupting" influence of the secular state, as well as to foster legitimacy for the Islamic movement through tangible provisions to the public. The Iranian revolution in 1979 and the liberation of Afghanistan from Soviet forces in the late 1980s reinforced the trend toward Islamic resurgence and activism as Islamists appeared to be effective agents of social change.[4]

Palestinian society did not escape this phenomenon. Significant segments of Palestinians living in the West Bank and Gaza have become more religious as a result of Islamic revivalism.[5] The rise of Hamas as a viable competitor of the nationalist camp in 1988, the success of the Islamic bloc in various universities in the West Bank and Gaza since the 1980s, and the proliferation of Islamic charity networks, especially in Gaza, created resources and a palpable legitimacy for the Islamic movement.[6] Although Fatah remained the dominant organization representing Palestinian aspirations for independence, the stock of Hamas rose quickly during the first uprising.

We cannot draw a straight causal line between religious revivalism and suicide bombings, however. Islamic fundamentalism created a context in which religious appeals and symbolism resonate much more readily than in previous decades. Whereas in the 1950s and 1960s religious groups were marginalized by the spirit and policies of secular nationalism, socialism, and Nasserism (after President Gamal Abdel Nasser of Egypt), since the 1980s religious interpretations of the multiple crises facing the Muslim world have gained privileged legitimacy among the wider public. Militant Palestinian factions find in Islamic revivalism a cultural opportunity that allows them to frame their suicide attacks as fulfillment of sacred imperatives to fight injustice.

Hamas and Islamic Jihad, the two main organizers of suicide attacks since the early 1990s, employ five means by which they link self-sacrifice to Islamic identities. First, Hamas and Islamic Jihad insist that jihad in Palestine is an individual obligation *(fard ayn)* as opposed to a collective obligation *(fard kifaya)*. Islamic scholars construe individual obligation to mean that it is the duty of every Muslim to wage jihad in the path of God in defense of Islam, its lands, religious institutions, people, and property. Individual obligation usually arises when Muslim lands are besieged by powerful foes that cannot be easily repelled with a small force. Under these circumstances, jihad is the religious obligation of every Muslim capable of fighting, just as all Muslims are obligated to pray, fast, and pay alms. In contrast, collective obligation means that the duty of jihad on individual Muslims is fulfilled if a sufficient number of Muslims arise to make additional fighters unnecessary for the task. Collective obligation usually applies in campaigns of conquest *(fatuhat)* that Muslims are powerful enough to undertake without the need to burden all of society.

Islamists in Palestine maintain that Islamic lands have been stolen by the Jews in alliance with powerful Western forces. Given the magnitude of the injustice, it is an individual obligation on every Muslim inside and outside Palestine to wage a jihad of liberation. Hamas's position has been influenced by the writings and personal example of Sheikh Abdullah Yussuf Azzam, a Palestinian who dedicated his earlier life to fighting against Israel and, later, against Soviet forces in Afghanistan. Although the current military wing of Hamas calls itself the "Militias of the Martyr Izzedin al-Qassam," which was the title of its armed groups in Gaza before the official formation of Hamas's military wing in January 1992, Hamas militants in the West Bank carried the title "Militias of Abdullah Azzam." When the Gaza and West Bank military wings joined together, there was a debate about whether to keep the West Bank wing's title in honor of Sheikh Azzam.[7] Azzam wrote a pamphlet titled "Defense of Muslim Lands: The First Obligation after Faith." In the fifty-two-page pamphlet, which consists of an introduction, four short chapters, and concluding remarks, he argues that all the Qur'anic commentators and scholars of all four Islamic legal traditions (Maliki, Hanafi, Shafai, and Hanbali) agree that when Muslim lands are threatened, *jihad* under this condition becomes a personal religious obligation *[fard ayn]* upon the Muslims of the land which the infidels have attacked and upon the Muslims close by, where the children will march forth without the permission of their parents, the wife without the permission of her husband, and the debtor without the permission of the creditor. And, if the Muslims of this land cannot expel the infidels because the lack of forces, because they are dragging, are indolent or simply do not act, then the individual obligation spreads in the shape of a circle from the nearest to the next nearest. If they too are dragging or there is again a shortage of manpower, then it is upon the people behind them, and on the people behind them, to march forward. This process continues until it becomes a personal religious obligation upon the whole world.[8]

This notion of jihad as an individual obligation is also proclaimed by Fathi al-Shiqaqi, one of the founders of the Palestinian Islamic Jihad.[9] It also received support from the popular Sheikh Yussuf al-Qardaqwi and many other Islamic scholars, as we shall see below.

The second means by which Hamas and Islamic Jihad seek to substantiate their claim for the necessity of sacrifice in Palestine is to draw on the abundant Islamic texts concerning jihad and martyrdom in the Qur'an and prophetic traditions. These passages urge Muslims to fight persecution and injustice in the path of God and not to fear death, because those killed in battle will be rewarded by God.[10] A systematic reading of the communiqués from Hamas and Islamic Jihad, in which they claim responsibility for attacks and present the last wills and testaments of the bombers, reveals that each communiqué invariably begins with one or more Qur'anic verses that either urge Muslims to embrace God's command to carry out jihad in the path of Allah and strike at the enemy without concern for one's own weaker military status or expound on the benefits of martyrdom:

2:154 — And call not those who are slain in the way of Allah "dead." Nay, they are living, only ye perceive not.

4:69 — Whoso obeyeth Allah and the messenger, they are with those unto whom Allah hath shown favor, of the Prophets and the saints and the martyrs and the righteous. The best of company are they!

8:17 — So you slew them not but Allah slew them, and thou smotest not when thou didst smite (the enemy), but Allah smote (him), and that He might confer upon the believers a benefit from Himself. Surely Allah is Hearing, Knowing.

9:14 — Fight them; Allah will chastise them at your hands and bring them to disgrace, and assist you against them and relieve the hearts of a believing people.

9:111 — Surely Allah has bought from the believers their persons and their property—theirs (in return) is the Garden. They fight in Allah's way, so they slay and are slain.

61:10–12 — O ye who have believed, shall I point you to a trade which will save you from a punishment painful? Ye should believe in Allah and His messenger, and should strive for the cause of Allah with your wealth and your lives. That is better for you, if ye did but know. He will forgive you your sins and bring you into Gardens underneath which rivers flow, and pleasant dwellings in Gardens of Eden. That is the supreme triumph.

In addition to these Qur'anic verses, many prophetic traditions venerate martyrdom in the path of God. The Prophet Muhammad describes jihad as the "pinnacle of faith" *(sinam al-din)*. In one hadith (prophetic saying), the Prophet Muhammad is reported to have said that "no slave [of God] who dies and has goodness with God wants to return to the world, even if he would have the world and all that is in it, except the martyr, for when he sees the greatness of martyrdom, he will want to return to the world and be killed again." In another, the Prophet Muhammad is said to have been approached by a man who asked him, "Where am I, Apostle of God, if I am killed [in battle?]" The Prophet replied, "heaven." The man "threw away the dates that were in his hand and fought [in battle] until he was killed."[11] According to the prophetic tradition, the benefits of martyrdom include the following:

❖ Remission of one's sins at the moment the martyr's blood is shed.

❖ Immediate admission into heaven, so martyrs do not suffer the punishment of the tomb.

❖ The privilege of accompanying prophets, saints, and righteous believers.

❖ Marriage to heavenly maidens *(houri al-ayn)*.

❖ The right to intercede with God on behalf of seventy relatives.

❖ Protection against the pain of death.

❖ Entry into the highest gardens of heaven *(jannat al-firdaous)*.

To be sure, the Qur'anic verses and prophetic traditions are subject to competing interpretations; they cannot serve as justifications for suicide bombings without the mediation of authoritative interpretation. Nonetheless, Hamas and Islamic Jihad present many of these texts as unproblematic grounds for suicide attacks, even against civilians. As we shall see below, their views have been given legitimacy by religious authorities inside and outside Palestine, thus making it difficult to contest their interpretations.

The third means that Hamas and Islamic Jihad use to link self-sacrifice to Islamic identities is to draw on the narrative of faith and persecution that characterized the prophetic career of Muhammad. In the first twelve years of his mission, beginning in AD 610, the Prophet Muhammad preached monotheism to the polytheists of Mecca. He endured ridicule and per-secution without calling for a violent jihad against his oppressors. When the danger against the embryonic Islamic community of Mecca grew to an unbearable level, the Prophet Muhammad and his followers left for the town of Yathrib (or al-Medina al-Munawara). In the ten years that fol-lowed, until the death of Muhammad in AD 632, the Muslims were given permission first to fight back against the onslaught of Meccan invasions and later to take the initiative against the unbelievers.[12] Despite being initially outnumbered, the Muslim community in Medina was able to stave off the superior Meccan forces and ultimately triumph over them. Had the first Islamic community succumbed to persecution, Islam as a world civilization would have died in its infancy. The dominant symbolism of this narrative is the defeat of unjust authority by dispossessed, righteous victims who did not recoil in the face of martyrdom and who relied on their faith to help them triumph over a superior enemy.

In interviews with members of the Islamic Bloc (generally Hamas supporters) at al-Najah University in Nablus and Bir Zeit University in Ramallah, I made it a point to ask about the wisdom of militarizing the uprising and deploying suicide bombers against the powerful Israeli state, which has not shown any willingness to give an inch in the face of Palestinian violence. Invariably, someone fires back that the early Islamic community of Medina faced a similarly powerful enemy, yet they prevailed despite the odds, because they had something stronger than guns, tanks, and fighter planes; they had faith and a love for the afterlife. It is interesting to note that one of the Qur'anic passages most cited by suicide bombers is from verse 8:17 (So you slew them not but Allah slew them). This verse comes from the battle of Badr, which was the first major battle between the Muslims of Medina and the invading Meccan army of about 1,000 men. Although the Muslims could muster only 314 fighters, the verse speaks of direct divine intervention to aid the Muslims, which was God's way of showing his blessings upon the faithful. Indeed, God sent angels from heaven to fight alongside the Muslims. Militants frame their contemporary struggle against Israel as part and parcel of the Islamic tradition of jihad and martyrdom by the weak against the strong, the righteous over the unjust.

The fourth tactic used by Hamas and Islamic Jihad is to circumvent the suicidal aspect of human bombings by euphemistic labeling. Instead of calling their operations "suicide bombings" *(tafjirat intihariyya)*, they term them "martyrdom operations" *(amaliyat istishhadiyya)*, because in Islam, as in other Abrahamic traditions, there are strict prohibitions against suicide. Sheikh Ahmed Yassin, the founder and assassinated leader of Hamas, when asked about the permissibility of committing suicide in an operation, replied, "If there are individuals that claim these operations are suicide, there are hundreds that say they are martyrdom."[13] He and others insist that suicide is about escapism, the deviation of weak minds. Martyrdom, on the other hand, is about noble sacrifice by strong-willed individuals. Suicide is the pathetic end to depression and despair; martyrdom is a new beginning for hope and deliverance. Suicide is shameful and something to be discouraged; martyrdom is honorable and worth emulating. Indeed, organizers of suicide bombings honor the mothers and fathers of "martyrs" by giving them the title of *"umm al-shahid"* (mother of the martyr) or *"abu al-shahid"* (father of the martyr), instead of *"umm Ahmad"* or *"abu Omar."* Such honor is not conferred on those who commit nonpolitical suicide. With the emphasis on martyrdom as opposed to suicide, it becomes very difficult to criticize the bombers directly. One may question the goals and tactics of their organizations, just as one may question the policies of states at war, but one rarely questions the heroism of individual martyrs, just as societies rarely question the gallantry of their fallen soldiers. Iyad Sarraj, a Palestinian psychiatrist, perhaps put it best: "You can say, 'I condemn terror,

I condemn killing civilians,' but you can't say, 'I condemn martyrs,' because martyrs are prophets."[14]

The fifth means employed by organizers of suicidal violence is to use ritual and ceremony to amplify the value of martyrdom in society. Ritual is symbolic behavior and prescribed procedure that is dramatic, socially standardized, and repetitive. It aims at arousing emotions, deepening commitments, and inculcating the values of collective ethos. It links individuals with broader goals and identities and may even link worldly time with sacred history. Ceremony is a formal, public ritual to commemorate a special event, celebrate human accomplishments, and honor solemn occasions with reverence. Setting apart an occasion or persons for special recognition implies social acceptance and veneration of one's action, position, or identity. Ceremony is intended as much for those observing the honor as for those honored. It is society's stamp of approval, one way of setting standards for action.[15]

Proponents of suicide bombings create posters, Web sites, and public exhibits to honor their "martyrs" and publicize their "heroic" sacrifice. At al-Najah University in Nablus, a place that has produced many suicide bombers, I saw posters and murals for "martyrs" exhibited on nearly every wall and entrance. This is also the case through the numerous towns, villages, and refugee camps of the West Bank and Gaza. One can hardly walk or drive without coming across the posters of the "martyrs" or their names written in graffiti style on the walls. Sermons are dedicated to commemorate the lives of the bombers and speak of their virtues.

Ritual and ceremony permeate all aspects of preparing "living martyrs" (suicide bombers in waiting) and burying dead ones. The videotape to record the last wills and testaments of the bombers and solidify their commitment to martyrdom; the white shrouds that cover the bombers from head to toe to symbolize both their purity and their preparedness for the grave; the headband and banners emblazoned with Qur'anic verses to decorate the living martyrs' quarters before they declare their intention to go on a mission; the guns and bombs that serve as props for their last photos, to symbolize empowered individuals making a free choice to self-sacrifice for the cause; the mass procession to commemorate the death of the martyr, often featuring other militants dressed as martyrs in waiting and strapped with fake explosive belts; the chants, from marchers and loudspeakers during burial processions, of *"bil rouh, bil damm, nafdika ya shahid"* (With our soul, with our blood, we sacrifice for you, o martyr); the melodramatic music to celebrate the heroism and sacrifice of the martyrs; the mourning ceremony, wherein the women ululate and distribute candy or sweet coffee to celebrate the martyr's entry into heaven, and the men receive congratulatory handshakes because their sons or daughters have achieved eternal salvation; the posters on a wall, and electronic links on a Web site to immortalize the bombers—all these actions are undertaken repeatedly, routinely, and with procedural rigor. These practices idealize the act of martyrdom and elevate its underlying values in the eyes of potential recruits, to inspire future missions. Ritual and ceremony imbue acts of extreme violence with meaning, purpose, and morality. Violence becomes a vehicle for upholding one's religious values and proving one's self-worth. It transforms cruel terror into sacred missions in the minds of potential militants and their sympathetic observers.

Ritual and ceremony have many powerful effects on recruitment—not directly, but by fostering an image of a heroic martyr that inspires others to emulate the dead bombers. Rituals and ceremonies

❖ engender identification between individuals and organizations, communicating a collective ethos in an emotional way in order to appeal to our visceral senses, not our intellect;

❖ simplify complex political realities by creating narratives of good and evil, right and wrong, honorable and disgraceful;

❖ elevate the status of some individuals over others, asserting that a person or category of persons is to be exalted;

❖ build solidarity without necessarily building consensus—they are inherently ambiguous, allowing people to affix different meanings to them;

❖ connect seemingly mundane worldly struggles with sacred time and history; and

❖ in the case of public rites, break the monotony of everyday routine, creating social incentives for participation and drawing people into a network of activists.

These five strategies for linking self-sacrifice to Islamic identities have fostered a culture of martyrdom that legitimizes self-immolation. Consequently, the religious framing of suicide bombings permeates many of the last wills and testaments of the suicide bombers. Groups such as Hamas and Islamic Jihad choose bombers who exhibit deep religious commitment, partly because the discourse of heavenly rewards associated with martyrdom depends on a sincere belief in God and the afterlife.[16]

The statements of the bombers reveal at least three themes. The first is their insistence that "martyrdom operations" are necessary to fulfill one's commitment to God and the Prophet Muhammad, who urged Muslims to fight persecution and not fear death. Suicide bombers emphasize the need to embrace martyrdom in order to achieve liberation, end injustice, seek vengeance, or fulfill one's duty to country and God. Ismail al-Masoubi, a suicide bomber who killed 2 Israelis and injured 1 in Gaza on June 22, 2001, wrote in his last will and testament, "Love for jihad and martyrdom has come to possess my life, my being, my feelings, my heart, and my senses. My heart ached when I heard the Quranic verses, and my soul was torn when I realized my shortcomings and the shortcomings of Muslims in fulfilling our duty toward fighting in the path of God almighty." Mahmoud Sleyman Abu Hasanein, who was bent on achieving martyrdom and who was killed in a nonsuicide attack in March 2002, wrote to his father, "Dear Father: If I do not defend my religion, my land and holy sites, and another person does not, and another, then who will liberate the land and the holy places?" It is important to note that this discourse is not limited to Hamas and Islamic Jihad bombers. The AMB uses the same Islamist discourse in its last wills and testaments. Abdel Salam Hasouna, a member of the AMB, begins his last will and testament with the following words: "After placing my trust in God almighty, and with faithful intentions toward the Lord of the world, I yearn for meeting God . . . I give myself in the path of God and for the sake of the two domes, and the third noble sanctuary, which is the gateway of our great Prophet. [I give myself] to continue the march of our venerable martyrs that have superseded us in their faith so that the word of God reigns supreme and the word of the infidels is low." Dareen Abu Ayshe, another AMB bomber, writes in her last will and testament, "Because the role of the Muslim Palestinian woman is no less important than the role of our fighting brothers, I have decided to be the second female martyr to continue in the path that was forged by the female martyr Wafa al-Idris. I give my humble self in the path of God to avenge the limbs of our martyred brothers and in revenge for the sanctity of our religion and mosques, and in revenge for the sanctity of the Aqsa mosque and all of God's places of worship that have been turned into [alcohol] bars in which all that has been forbidden by God is pursued in order to spite our religion and to insult the message of our Prophet."

The second theme that emerges from the discourse of suicide bombers and their supporters is the redemptive act of martyrdom. Suicide bombing is not only an opportunity to punish an enemy and fulfill God's command to fight injustice but also a privilege and a reward to those most committed to their faith and their values. To be selected for "martyrdom operations" is akin to receiving a stamp of approval or a certificate of accomplishment from one's peers. It is a form of endorsement of one's moral character and dedication. Hiba Daraghmeh, a female suicide bomber dispatched by Islamic Jihad, killed 3 Israelis and wounded 70 on May 19, 2003. When her family inquired about her upbeat mood the day before the attack, she told them, "I feel that I am a new person. You will be very proud of me."[17] I encountered many stories or statements of bombers that refer to their missions euphemistically as "a test" or a challenge to prove their courage and manhood. Fouad Ismail al-Hourani, who blew himself up on March 9, 2002, killing 11 Israelis and injuring 54, wrote in his last will and testament, "Can there be men of truth if we are not (willing to be) men? A believer without courage is like a tree without fruit." The mother of Abdel Muti Shabana, who carried out a bombing on June 1, 2003, killing 17 Israelis and injuring over 100, tells of how, on the day of the operation, her son asked her repeatedly to pray that God make him successful in his upcoming test. (She thought he was referring to a school examination.)

Moreover, the act of martyrdom is seen as an attempt to redeem society of its failure to act righteously. Words expressed by revered martyrs carry a great deal of weight. Thus, some suicide bombers use their statements to express their view of how individuals and communities should act to overcome the malaise that characterizes their condition. Some urge their mothers, fathers, brothers, and sisters to pray regularly (especially the dawn prayers), to wear the *hijab*, and to be among the best Muslims on earth. Shadi Sleyman al-Nabaheen, who carried out a suicide mission on

May 19, 2003, wrote in his last will and testament, "My dear brothers and sisters: Forgive me for any mistake or lapse in judgment toward you . . . I urge you to be supportive of my mother and father and do not fall short [of your duty] toward them . . . Be from among the patient and steadfast and hold tightly to the religion of God. Guide your children to the mosque and instruct them to read the Quran and attend the recitation lessons, and teach them to love jihad and martyrdom." Mahmoud Siyam, a member of the AMB, writes in his last will and testament, "Mother . . . Father, I urge you to pray and fast, to recite and chant the Lord's name, and entreat God to have mercy on me and forgive me. I ask you to be pleased with me and ask God for mercy on my behalf. I know I will leave a void in your lives, but this is the calling of my God and my nation."

Others use their martyrdom to urge fellow Muslims to follow in their example in order to redeem Muslims in their moment of weakness. Shadi Sleyman al-Nabaheen declared in his last will and testament, "The tree of Islam is continuously nourished with the blood of martyrs so that it can provide shade to those who come after us." He rhetorically asks fellow Muslims around the world, "How long will the Muslim nation continue in its stupor and paralysis? . . . I say to you [Muslims] we are coming from the midst of the pile [of fallen martyrs], we will arise from our wounds and limbs, for a pure and virtuous Muslim youth took upon themselves the burden of their nation to get rid of its oppression in order to raise high in the sky its banner 'There is no God but Allah, and Muhammad is His Prophet.'" Jihad Walid Hamada, who carried out an operation on August 4, 2002, killing 9 Israelis and injuring 40, is equally eloquent in his last will and testament: "May our blood become a lantern that lights up for those around us the path towards liberation, to raise the banner of truth, the banner of Islam."

The third theme that emerges is that of reward in the afterlife. Kamal Abdelnasser Rajab, an Islamic Jihad suicide bomber, cites the following prophetic tradition in his last will and testament: "In heaven, God has prepared 100 ranks for those holy fighters that fight in His path. The difference between one level and another is akin to the difference between heaven and earth." He goes on to declare: "O father and mother, dearest to my heart; o brothers, sisters, and friends, life near God is the best of lives and better than life itself, especially one dominated by arrogant tyrants." Suicide bombers also speak of heavenly rewards for their families. In many communiqués they ask their mothers and fathers to forgive them and remind them that God has promised martyrs the privilege of interceding on behalf of seventy family members on Judgment Day. Hamed Abu Hejleh, a suicide bomber who blew himself up at a bus stop in Netanya in January 2001, injuring 60 Israelis, tells his family in his last will and testament, "If I have fallen short in my duty toward you in this world, I will not fall short during Judgment Day, God willing. For know that the Prophet Muhammad, peace be upon him, has said that the martyr intercedes [with God] on behalf of seventy of his family members." Shadi Sleyman al-Nabaheen wrote to his mother and father in his last will and testament: "I wanted to beat you to heaven so I can intercede with my God on your behalf."

Suicide bombers urge their families to celebrate rather than mourn their "martyrdom" after a suicidal mission, to rejoice in their entry into heaven. The previously mentioned suicide bomber Hamed Abu Hejleh, whose oversize picture was mounted in one of the main staircases at al-Najah University, where he studied civil engineering, wrote in his last will and testament, "My last wish to you my family is that none of you should weep in my procession to heaven. Indeed, distribute dates and ululate in the wedding of martyrdom." The mother of Muhammad Fathi Farhat, who was videotaped with her son before his operation, wishing him success, was also videotaped after he completed his mission, distributing sweets to neighbors who came to "celebrate." She reproached those who sobbed, asking them to leave because she would not accept tears on this joyous occasion.

NATIONALIST CONFLICT AND COMMUNITY TIES

The discourse of Hamas and Islamic Jihad is not purely religious; they, along with secular groups such as the AMB and the PFLP, draw on deep nationalist feelings to inspire people to die for the nation.[18] To be sure, the secular groups rely on the culture of martyrdom fostered by the Islamists. Similarly, many of the suicide bombers of Hamas and Islamic Jihad reference nationalist goals and desire for defiance and revenge in the face of repressive Israeli measures. It would be a mistake, therefore, to claim that the bombers of Hamas and Islamic Jihad rely on religious motivations, while the bombers of the AMB and the PFLP rely on nationalism; the motives of the bombers are much more complex and interwoven.

One theme that emerges from a systematic reading of statements made by bombers is their desire to shake Palestinians in particular as well as Muslims and Arabs in general into action by a drastic act of heroism. Muhammad Hazza al-Ghoul, a Hamas member who blew himself up on a bus on June 18, 2002, killing 19 Israelis and injuring 52, wrote in his last will and testament, "How beautiful for the splinters of my bones to be the response that blows up the enemy, not for the love of killing, but so we can live as other people live. . . . We do not sing the songs of death, but recite the hymns of life. . . . We die so that future generations may live." This theme of sacrifice for the sake of others is echoed in the eulogy given to two suicide bombers from Nablus by Qais Adwan, a Hamas organizer of suicide attacks killed by Israelis in April 2002: "It's amazing that man sacrifices himself so as to enable his nation to live."[19]

The symbolism of martyrdom is seen as perhaps sufficient to awaken the consciousness of Arab nations to compel their governments to act in unison against Israel and its allies. Muhammad al-Habashi, who blew himself up on September 9, 2001, killing 3 Israelis and injuring 90, wrote in his last will and testament, "I ask God almighty that my martyrdom is a message to all the Arab and Muslim nations to get rid of the injustice of their rulers that weigh heavily on their shoulders, and to rise to bring victory to Muslims in Jerusalem and Palestine, and in all conquered Muslim lands." Mahmoud Sleyman Abu Hasanein, mentioned earlier, concludes his last will and testament with words directed toward all Arab and Muslim nations of the world: "Why are you committed to this transient world? Why the fear? We only die once, so let it be for the sake of God." Ayat Akhras, a female suicide bomber who blew herself up in a Jerusalem supermarket in March 2002, killing a bodyguard and a young woman nearly her age, declared in her videotaped message, "I am going to fight instead of the sleeping Arab armies who are watching Palestinian girls fight alone."

Nationalism is as much about an imagined community as it is about shared borders, language, and culture. Imagined community, following Benedict Anderson, refers to how members of disparate communities come to identify themselves as a unified nation despite the fact that they have never met and are not likely ever to know one another on a personal level.[20] Others refer to this phenomenon as fictive kin, whereby individuals who do not know one another personally develop emotional ties based on social identification, especially in times of crisis or trauma.[21] The events of September 11 undoubtedly generated such feelings among Americans, who grieved together regardless of whether they lost loved ones in the tragic attacks of that day.

Israel's response to Palestinian violence generated additional grievances, humiliations, and traumas that resulted in a desire among ordinary people to avenge loved ones as well as those they identified with on a personal level. Closures, curfews, checkpoints, home demolitions, targeted assassinations, military incursions, and the security barrier/wall of separation had a dual effect of building bonds of solidarity among communities and increasing the desire for defiance and vengeance.[22] Daily killings that were televised by local and satellite media resulted in a "multiplier effect," in which the pain of one community reverberated in other communities. Many Palestinian bombers insist that their violence is a response to the overwhelming injustices perpetrated by Israeli forces. If the Israelis did not kill old men, women, and children, the Palestinians would not be compelled to attack Israeli civilians in retaliation, they argue. Jamal Abdel-Ghani Nasser, a suicide bomber who carried out an operation on April 29, 2001, killing no one but himself, wrote this message before his mission: "Who amongst us was not enraged and did not seek vengeance when witnessing the mothers, wives, and sons and daughters of the martyrs on television; who from among us did not feel as one of the homeowners that had their homes destroyed lately in Khan Yunis and Rafah; who amongst us did not feel rage when children were killed, trees uprooted, and towns bombarded?" Mahmoud Ahmad Marmash, who carried out a suicide attack on May 18, 2001, killing 5 Israelis and injuring over 100 in Netanya, begins his last will and testament with these words: "The Palestinian people are encountering the cruelest times, enduring daily killings, bombardment, displacement, and the most extreme forms of violence. Every day its suffering increases. A group must arise to sacrifice itself and strive in the path of God to defend its honor and its people." In an investigative report by the *Guardian* newspaper, the friends and families of 21 suicide bombers were interviewed. It was reported that all the families described the bombers as being influenced emotionally by daily images of killings, sometimes "breaking down in tears or shouting before their television sets."[23]

Perhaps one of the better-known stories is that of the twenty-seven-year-old apprentice lawyer Hanadi Jaradat, one of the female suicide bombers of Islamic Jihad. On October 4, 2003, she blew herself up in the Maxim restaurant in the Israeli seaside town of Haifa, killing 21 Israelis and injuring 60. Like Hiba Daraghmeh before her, she, too, appeared to her family to be happy the day before the attack. There can be little doubt about what motivated her action. Four months before, her twenty-three-year-old brother Fadi and her thirty-one-year-old cousin, both members of Islamic Jihad, were killed in Israeli military actions. After those deaths, she became radicalized. She was always intensely religious, but the killings of her brother and cousin, along with the refusal of Israeli military authorities in Jenin to grant her father a permit for medical treatment in Haifa for his liver ailment, resulted in deep trauma. Her mother reports that she "was full of pain. . . . She saw them taking the body [of her brother] from the hospital to the morgue, and she was different after that. Some nights, she woke up screaming, saying she had nightmares about Fadi." The reaction of her family reflects how community ties could lay the basis for societal support for suicide attacks, a theme that will be taken up in the next section. Her mother told reporters, "She has done what she has done, thank God, and I am sure that what she has done is not a shameful thing, she has done it for the sake of her people." Her father had a similar reply: "I don't want to talk about my feelings, my pain, my suffering. But I can tell you that our people believe that what Hanadi has done is justified. Imagine yourself watching the Israelis kill your son, your nephew, destroying your house . . . they are pushing our people into a corner, they are provoking actions like these by our people."[24]

Nicole Argo, a PhD candidate at MIT, conducted interviews with foiled Palestinian suicide bombers in Israeli prisons. She illustrates how feelings of community were expressed in the motivations of the would-be bombers.[25] Here is a sample from five suicide bombers reflecting on their motives:

> I didn't decide in one moment [to carry out an attack]. I had been thinking about it from the beginning of the Intifada, looking for an opportunity and an organization to help me do it. There were few factors affecting the

decision—the stress of the occupation, the humiliation of my cousin being searched by soldiers, the killings . . . against kids—and the action was in honor of the kids who were killed.

I did this because of the suffering of the Palestinian people. The falling of *shuhada* [those martyred by Israeli forces] . . . and the destruction everywhere in Palestine . . . I did this for God and for the Palestinian people.

I didn't think about the consequences of the operation—if it would make things better or not. I don't understand politics . . . but that we are able to react against their bombings and their killing of inhabitants of the camp is important. My mission made them [in the camp] happy, even though they were punished a lot [for it] in Jenin. The land and trees and houses were punished; nothing remains that they did not punish.

I believe the operation would hurt the enemy . . . Also [a] successful mission greatly influences society. It raises the morale of the people; they are happy, they feel strong.

I know the bombing will hurt the Israelis and prove to them that we are still ready to fight. [So much] happened to our camp because of the destruction—someone told me the operation would be a benefit to the camp, to create pressure on the Israelis in order that they retreat from the territory. . . . The most important thing was that we should make an operation in the heart of Israel after the [Israeli military] penetration in order to prove that we were not influenced by the military attack.

All these statements reflect the underlying sense of moral righteousness derived from the act of self-sacrifice. They also show that one cannot simply disaggregate nationalism and religious revivalism; the suicide bombers are dying for God and country. Religious revivalism, nationalist conflict, and community ties underpin the culture of martyrdom that emerged during the second Palestinian uprising. Organizations drew on these three sources of identity to engender the myth of the heroic martyr. These identities were interwoven by militant groups to frame martyrdom as an act of redemption, empowerment, and defiance against unjust authorities. Volunteers for suicide attacks are not brainwashed victims of opportunistic organizations, nor are they manipulated individuals who are fooled by calculating terrorists. Instead, it is more appropriate to say that they are *inspired* by the opportunity to fulfill their obligation to God, sacrifice for the nation, and avenge a grieving people. These motivations are not the same as the strategic calculations of the organizers of suicide attacks. Nor are they sufficient to explain why societies venerate suicide bombers. The question that remains to be answered is, what explains the depth of societal support for this strategy of martyrdom? Why were the radicals able to convince the broader public of the appropriateness of suicide bombings?

5

SOCIETAL MOTIVES
The Logic of Communities in Conflict

Societies under normal conditions do not embrace and venerate suicidal violence. Extreme violence usually follows previous cycles of low-intensity violence that polarize communities and foster feelings of victimization. In the case of the Palestinians, two conditions converged to make suicidal violence honorable in society: (1) Communities felt a deep sense of victimization by external enemies in the course of political conflict, and (2) legitimate authorities promoted or acquiesced to extreme violence. To understand these dynamics, we must first understand the factors that contributed to the militarization of the al-Aqsa Intifada, because the use of force by each side in the initial stages of the uprising contributed to polarization and feelings of victimization.

FROM STONES TO GUNS: COMPARING THE TWO INTIFADAS

Why did the Palestinians use guns and human bombs in the al-Aqsa Intifada when they could have used more peaceful means to confront the Israeli occupation? During the first Palestinian uprising (1987–93), Palestinian youth won the sympathy of the world and focused international attention on their plight by mere rock throwing against the Israeli occupation forces. When they relied on demonstrations, strikes, boycotts, and civil disobedience, they won over international public opinion and forced the Israeli mainstream to question the morality of occupation. Ultimately, the sacrifices of rock-throwing youth contributed to the start of the peace process and recognition of Palestinian national aspirations, which had been denied by previous Israeli governments. Why did the Palestinians not do the same in the second uprising?

These are critical questions that go to the heart of who is to blame for the bloodshed in the second Palestinian uprising. Answers to these questions help explain how dynamics of violence could grow out of structural factors that are beyond the control of individuals, organizations, or states. Five crucial differences between the two intifadas help explain the Palestinians' turn to arms in the opening days and weeks of the second uprising. First, weapons were much more widespread in the second uprising than in the first. Before the first uprising, Israelis were suspicious of anyone possessing arms, especially automatic weapons that could be turned against them. Palestinians with guns had to be careful because the consequences of being caught were severe. Israelis confiscated weapons from Palestinians whenever they found them and often imprisoned those who were in possession of arms, especially if they were members of banned Palestinian factions, such as Fatah or the PFLP. When the first uprising broke out, therefore, weapons were difficult to acquire. In addition, before the first intifada, the Palestinians naturally did not have thousands of security forces trained in the use of firearms. As a result, Palestinians were forced to adhere to peaceful or quasi-violent tactics such as stone throwing and firebombings using Molotov cocktails. The situation changed after the Oslo peace process. Although estimates of the size of the PA security services during the Oslo years vary, no one questions that more than 40,000 Palestinians were armed as members of the official police force, security services, or armed militias within Fatah's Tanzim.[1] Thus, when the second uprising broke out, the Palestinians had the necessary resources for militarizing the conflict. Almost from the opening days of the uprising, Palestinian militias did not refrain from using guns, either to shoot at Israeli soldiers who were firing at demonstrators or to fire randomly at nearby settlements.

Second, the geography of confrontation in the al-Aqsa uprising was drastically different from that in the first intifada. In the first uprising, Israeli forces were well entrenched in Palestinian towns. They patrolled them day and night and entered them regularly for searches and arrests and to enforce curfews. Palestinians did not have to look far to find the occupation forces. As a result, friction with the Palestinian populace was an ever-present possibility, and clashes, when they broke out, took place in the heart of Palestinian towns and villages. Palestinians did not have to march a long distance or drive far to confront Israeli soldiers. The Oslo peace process changed the geography of confrontation. The segmentation of the Palestinian territories into areas A, B, and C had important implications for future conflicts. Area A was under complete Palestinian administrative and security jurisdiction. Area B was under Palestinian administrative jurisdiction, but Israel was responsible for security matters. Area C was under complete Israeli administrative and security jurisdiction.

When the second uprising began, the majority of Palestinians in the territories were living under full PA administration. However, the redeployment of Israeli forces from the major towns and cities of the West Bank was accompanied by a system of checkpoints from one area to another and near Israeli settlements and around holy sites. This system of segmentation meant that confrontations between Israelis and Palestinians were less fluid. Instead, they took place at fixed points where the Israeli forces had the advantage of distance, open space, and fortified positions. Whereas in the first uprising Israeli soldiers were often taken by surprise when young men and women threw stones at passing patrols, sometimes from building tops or from narrow streets and alleyways, in the second uprising Israeli forces saw Palestinian protesters coming, accompanied by Palestinian militias and security services carrying arms. This made the Palestinians appear aggressive, as if they were looking for a fight, which undoubtedly contributed to a strong Israeli reaction to repel demonstrators, including the use of snipers and lethal bullets. It also made Israelis appear to be deliberately shooting to kill since they were behind fortified positions. It is one thing to shoot in reaction to rock throwers who surprise an Israeli patrol passing on foot in narrow alleyways, and quite another to take aim and shoot at demonstrators from afar with lethal bullets. Use of excessive force by Israelis, as we shall see below, contributed to feelings of rage among armed Palestinian security services and Fatah militiamen, resulting in immediate exchanges of fire.[2]

The initial dynamic of violence contributed to the third major difference between the two intifadas. Although the first intifada contributed to a high Palestinian casualty rate, the number of Palestinians killed and injured in the opening months of the second uprising was much higher and, as we shall see below, better televised. The use of Palestinian guns at fixed flash points meant that the technically inferior Palestinian forces were likely to bear the brunt of casualties. The IDF had the upper hand because it was able to limit the geography of confrontation and shield itself behind strategic positions and barriers that were well fortified and armed with snipers. The high casualty rate resulted in Palestinian calls for escalation to punish the Israelis for their use of excessive force.

The fourth major difference has to do with the media. In the first uprising, the Palestinians lacked independent presses and television newscasts that could escape Israeli censorship. Most of their news came from Israeli, Jordanian, and Egyptian news sources or from leaflets by underground committees. Although much of the Western world was able to see daily televised images of the first intifada, the Palestinian public and Arab viewers in the Middle East had limited access to these news reports and images. By the time of the second uprising, Palestinian and Arab viewers had access to satellite broadcasters such as al-Jazeera, al-Manar, and Abu Dhabi television. The Palestinians had ample televised news sources that were free of Israeli censorship. These networks provided around-the-clock coverage of events and were sympathetic solely with the Palestinian cause. Arab satellites served a dual role. They disseminated information on a day-to-day basis, thus raising the emotional intensity in the occupied territories following televised images of dead Palestinians. They also inspired Arab and Muslim protests around the world, which gave the Palestinians a sense that they were not alone in their rage. The media helped foster a community unified in pain and outrage at daily killings, resulting in a desire for vengeance.

The fifth major difference relates to leadership. The first uprising was a spontaneous explosion after twenty years of occupation; it took both Israel and the PLO by surprise. However, it did not take long for the PLO to play a major leadership role in the uprising, giving it organizational support and directing its day-to-day activities. With the exception of Hamas, the PLO unified the various factions into the United National Leadership for the Uprising (UNLU) in early 1988. It organized neighborhood committees and mobilized civil, labor, and professional associations to confront the occupation through peaceful means and acts of self-reliance and civil disobedience. It managed the tempo of events in the street. In the second intifada, the PA could not officially direct the day-to-day activities of the uprising because of its commitment to the Oslo peace process. Although Fatah cadres were in the lead in mobilizing confrontations with Israeli forces, PA and Fatah leaders did not lay out specific strategies and tactics to guide the uprising, lest they be implicated in the rebellion. Palestinian civil organizations were not active, and popular committees were not formed to coordinate civil disobedience. Labor unions, women's and teachers' organizations, student associations, and small businesses were not involved as extensively—and were not asked to be involved—as in the first uprising, because many such groups were incorporated into PA institutions. The PA sought to benefit from the uprising during the final-status phase of negotiations without officially claiming to take part in it. Yasser Arafat as the head of the PA could not decide, or perhaps did not want to decide, whether he was leading a resistance movement that aimed to mobilize people for national liberation or leading a national authority overseeing the emergence of a Palestinian state through negotiations. Thus, issues of strategy, tactics, and leadership were left to the discretion of disparate armed factions, many of which had competing viewpoints and interests. It was left up to the street to lead the uprising. To the extent that the PA leadership played a role, it was a reactive one in which it merely condemned certain episodes of violence or sought to deescalate the violence at key diplomatic junctures; it did not offer programmatic steps as an alternative to what was taking place on the ground.[3] As a result, events on the ground, not leadership decisions, controlled the tempo of the struggle.[4]

POLARIZING CONFLICTS AND PERCEIVED VICTIMIZATION

Societies embrace extreme violence when they perceive overwhelming threats to their security, identity, or national aspirations and when they see themselves solely as the victims. Stuart Kaufman explains this dynamic's role in the ethnic violence in Eastern Europe during the years following the collapse of the Soviet Union: "A fundamental factor causing ethnic conflicts to escalate to war is that first one side, then eventually both sides, come to fear that the existence of their group is at stake. Such extreme fears justify hostile attitudes toward the other group and extreme measures in self-defense, including demands for political dominance."[5] A progression of radicalization must take place before communities agree to support extreme violence. Without overwhelming threats and feelings of victimization—whether real or perceived—societies are likely to reject extreme violence against ordinary civilians.

In the case of the Palestinian-Israeli conflict, the initial rounds of violence, in the first few months of the uprising that began in September 2000, polarized the two nations as each side saw the other as unduly aggressive and brutal. The Palestinians repeatedly pointed out the high casualty rates suffered at the hands of Israeli forces. Dr. Mustafa Barghouti, who headed up the Palestinian Health, Development, Information and Policy Institute and who was a candidate for president of the Palestinian Authority, argues, "About 48 percent of those who died were shot in the head or neck. That means the soldiers shot to kill, as if they were anxious to prove their marksmanship and create a strong psychological effect. If you are in a life-threatening situation, you don't take your time to pinpoint the head." According to Barghouti, 319 Palestinians were killed in the first twelve weeks (September 29–December 18), 16 percent of whom were aged 15 or younger, 20 percent aged 16–18, 44 percent aged 19–29, 12 percent aged 30–39, and 8 percent aged over 40. Only 5 percent were killed in armed clashes, while 56.7 percent were killed in civilian demonstrations, and 4.1 percent were assassinated.[6] Ghassan al-Khatib, Palestinian minister of labor, attributes the militarization of the intifada to excessive force by the Israelis against civilian demonstrators and availability of arms to Palestinian factions. He points out that in the first ten days of the intifada, Israel killed a hundred Palestinian civilians, an average of ten per day, in addition to thirteen Arab-Israelis killed inside Israel. "Those people didn't carry arms, they were not on their way to carry out bomb attacks, they were only taking part in largely peaceful demonstrations, and only a few were throwing stones. Nonetheless, Israeli soldiers were ordered to shoot and kill those people. . . . All this shows that Israel drove us to resort to the armed intifada."[7]

As chart 4 indicates, during the first two months of the uprising, before suicide bombings were deployed by militant factions, the Palestinians bore the brunt of the casualties. Amnesty International summarized the events of the opening days of the uprising:

Confrontations took place at "symbolic areas"—where land had been confiscated, near checkpoints and on the way to Israeli settlements. The Amnesty International delegation found that the Israeli security forces, in policing the violent demonstrations, had tended to use military methods, rather than policing methods involving the protection of human lives. The security forces had moved swiftly from using non-lethal to lethal methods of control. They had breached their own rules of engagement that allow the use of firearms only when lives are in imminent danger, and then only targeted to the source of fire, and had used potentially lethal force randomly over a wide area.[8]

In interviews with members of the Fatah movement, I was repeatedly told that excessive use of force by the Israelis in the first two months of the uprising created conditions for the militarization of the conflict. As one militant told me, "The sons of your nation are being massacred. We couldn't fold our arms and stand there [and not shoot back]." Palestinians felt that conventional protest was inadequate in the face of such brutality. Many policemen in the Palestinian Authority were urged to "act like men" and shoot back at Israelis firing at stone-throwing protesters. As Israeli assassinations of militants escalated, so did the militants' desire to punish Israel with suicide bombings.[9]

From the Israeli perspective, the Palestinians—and Yasser Arafat in particular—turned to violence to achieve strategic aims after having pledged to renounce violence during the Oslo peace process. Moreover, the Palestinians used violence after the Israeli government was willing to make the most generous concessions in the history of peace negotiations between the two parties. Waging war on Israel during the final-status talks showed bad faith on the part of the Palestinians, and determination to gain advantages through violence. In the eyes of many Israelis, Arafat's turn to violence constituted a Machiavellian move to cover up his venal rule and lack of will to make genuine peace. Israelis were compelled to fend for themselves because of the PA's failure to halt the violence.[10] Finally, the Israelis argue that Palestinian protest was hardly peaceful when policemen armed by Israel turned their guns on Israeli soldiers. According to former deputy defense minister Ephraim Sneh, "If this level of violence had been maintained against any other army in the world, the death toll would have been at least 3,000, not 300."[11] If the Israelis had not responded with determined force, Palestinians would have seen this as a mark of weakness, which would have encouraged more violence.

Perceptions of victimization on each side in the opening rounds of fighting created an environment of insecurity, resulting in demands for an escalation in order to end the threats as well as punish the other side for acting unjustly. As the cycle of violence deepened, support for extreme measures began in earnest. Among the Palestinians, public opinion polls expressed greater support for suicide bombings against Israeli civilians. In March 1999, in the last poll taken by the Jerusalem Media and Communication Center before the uprising began, 26.1 percent of Palestinians supported suicide bombings against Israel; in December 2000, three months into the uprising, the percentage favoring such attacks had more than doubled, to 66.2 percent.

The Israeli response to Palestinian violence was equally violent. Aerial and naval attacks on Palestinian police stations and government institutions were seen as deliberate attempts to destroy the Palestinian Authority and the foundations of a future Palestinian state. Curfews, closures, and checkpoints at Palestinian villages, towns, and cities were seen as unfair collective punishments and an attempt to humiliate Palestinians in their own land. Targeted assassinations, home demolitions, and military incursions deepened feelings of victimization and widened calls for retaliation. Each Israeli attack was seen as a "massacre," and each Palestinian death was portrayed as a "war crime."

The ultimate Israeli response to Palestinian violence, however, was the election of Ariel Sharon as prime minister in February 2001. This constituted the most serious threat to Palestinian national aspirations. In the minds of many Palestinians, Sharon is not just a hawkish leader; he is an ideology and a symbol of Palestinian victimization. Sharon is regarded as a founder of hard-line policies in the occupied territories, the father of the settlement movement, and the defense minister responsible for the 1982 war in Lebanon and the subsequent ouster of the PLO from that bordering state. He is seen as a vociferous opponent of the Oslo accords and of a Palestinian state along the 1967 borders. Most of all, Sharon is associated with massacres of Palestinians in Sabra and Shatilla in 1982, when hundreds of defenseless civilians in Lebanese refugee camps perished at the hands of Christian militias under Israeli protection. Sharon's election meant that the peace process was likely to stagnate and all hopes for an independent Palestinian state in the West Bank and Gaza were likely to fade. In light of the apparent threat to their institutions and national aspirations, many Palestinians felt that extreme violence in the form of suicide bombings against a civilian population that had elected Sharon was justified.[12] In April 2001, a month after Sharon formed his government, support for suicide bombers had increased from 66.2 percent (December 2000) to 73.7 percent.[13] As chart 3 shows, Palestinian suicide bombings increased, quarter after quarter, following Sharon's rise to power, reaching their peak in March 2002.

The confluence of perceived threats and a sense of victimization plays a large part in explaining why Palestinian society came to venerate martyrdom. Suicide bombers assuaged two visceral reactions that stemmed from Israeli actions: revenge in response to perceived victimization at the hands of an "obstinate" enemy, and empowerment in the face of overwhelming threats by a superior adversary. Escalation by both sides to the conflict created a security dilemma wherein one's security depended on taking measures that deepened the insecurity of the other side.

LEGITIMIZING AUTHORITY

If Islam presented proponents of suicide bombings with a cultural opportunity to frame their deadly tactic as the highest form of martyrdom, the failure of the PA and authoritative religious figures to counter this framing of suicidal violence as martyrdom presented radicals with a political opportunity that facilitated their missions. Violence framed as a religiously sanctioned duty often encounters opposing voices based on competing interpretations of sacred texts and prophetic traditions. In the case of the Palestinians, however, the PA, which was in a position to do so, failed to adequately counter the radical ideology of Islamic militants, at times promoting a culture of martyrdom that was instrumental in recruiting suicide bombers. A number of studies have shown that recurring violence in ethnic conflict cannot take place without either the breakdown of state authority or the acquiescence of powerful government officials in command of the state's repressive capacity to prevent violent dissent.[14] As Kaufman explains, ethnic violence requires opportunity:

> Effective policing can prevent violent episodes from escalating, and political repression can prevent ethnic leaders from articulating their demands and mobilizing their followers for conflict. Therefore, as long as a state maintains an effective apparatus of repression and uses it to suppress ethnic mobilization, large-scale ethnic violence cannot occur.[15]

To be sure, the PA did not start the al-Aqsa uprising that began in September 2000, but it did very little to stop it. The PA, along with Arab satellite television broadcasters such as al-Jazeera, contributed to the legitimization of suicidal violence in four ways. First, Palestinian and other media continuously portrayed "martyrs"—whether militants killed in action or ordinary people who became fatalities in Israeli strikes—as heroic victims. News reports were unabashedly one-sided depictions of daily killings, which portrayed nearly every Israeli action as a "massacre," thus fostering deep feelings of victimization. Images of Palestinian youth dying by Israeli guns and of militants killed in action were not presented objectively; instead, they were accompanied by melodramatic music and nationalistic songs, at times by such renowned singers as Marcel Khalifa and Fayrouz, both of whom personalize the conflict with their poignant lyrics and powerful, extraordinary voices. Such reporting heightened emotions and venerated valiant death. Daphne Burdman explains:

> Music is a prominent feature, sometimes with a martial beat; gripping, pronouncedly rhythmic, maybe with a repetitive single drum-beat, sometimes triumphal, otherwise quiet, plaintive, nostalgic, then rising to a crescendo accompanying evocative lyrics. The chants are often of those heard at funeral processions for fallen Hamas and Islamic Jihad [martyrs]; underlying stirring martial connotations are unmistakable. In many places one hears, almost sub-threshold, buried in long stretches of music to the slow beat of the rhythm, repeated endlessly like a mantra, the quietly spoken word "shaheed" [martyr] . . . "shaheed" . . . "shaheed."[16]

Second, rather than speaking out unequivocally against suicide attacks that target civilians, the PA most often linked those attacks to the violence perpetrated by the Israelis against Palestinians. The usual condemnations of suicide attacks were phrased in the following manner: "We condemn all attacks against civilians, whether they are Israeli or Palestinian civilians. We call upon Israel and the international community to put an end to the conditions that breed violence against civilians." This manner of "condemning" attacks was widely understood by the Palestinian public as "mere diplomatic talk" forced on the PA by international pressure. Moreover, it actually served to justify suicide bombings by implying that they were directly linked to conditions that compelled people to blow themselves up. It was only in late 2001, following the September 11 attacks on the United States, that the PA began to speak out more consistently against suicide bombings. The real change of heart, however, took place in late 2002, in response to Israeli military incursions into Palestinian cities and towns. Many seasoned leaders within the PA began to question the utility of suicide bombings and of the militarization of the conflict in general. By that time, however, the cycle of violence was well beyond the PA's control.

Third, in the opening months of the uprising, the PA released many known militants who were connected to the suicide bombings of the mid-1990s. In doing so, they gave a "green light" to militant groups to carry out attacks without fear of retribution.[17] Fourth, the PA repeatedly refused to investigate attacks against Israeli civilians until international pressure forced it to do so in late 2001, in the aftermath of September 11. Even then, militants who were arrested were often released or actually kept under detention to protect them from Israeli assassinations.[18]

Palestinians often claim that Israeli military strikes on the institutions and security apparatuses of the PA reduced the PA's ability to fight suicide terrorism. This argument is not convincing. At a minimum, the PA had the physical capacity to arrest and prosecute known militants throughout the first year of the uprising. In the past, modest security measures by the PA signaled that it would not tolerate acts that jeopardized the peace process. As a result, armed groups restricted their activities to avoid sparking a civil war with the PA. Had the PA done the same in the opening months of the uprising, it could well have contained the violence. The actions by Mahmoud Abbas (Abu Mazen), following his election as the president of the PA in January 2005, show that the Palestinian security services had sufficient capacity to take tangible measures against the armed groups. Following his election, Abu Mazen insisted that the Palestinians cease firing rockets on Israeli settlements and towns. He placed Palestinian security forces in hot spots to prevent armed groups from launching rockets, resulting in a substantial decline in the number of rocket attacks.

Religious authorities inside and outside the Palestinian territories also spoke favorably about suicide attacks against Israeli civilians. Such support came not only from radical bastions of Islamism such as Iran, or Hezbollah in southern Lebanon, but also from traditionally conservative sources such as Egypt's al-Azhar.[19] Notable religious figures such as Sheikh Akrama Sabri, chief mufti of Jerusalem; Sheikh Ahmed al-Tayyeb, mufti of Egypt; Sheikh Muhammed Tantawi, imam al-Azhar in Egypt, all affirmed the right of Palestinians to carry out "martyrdom operations" against Israelis.[20] Most of all, Sheikh Yussuf al-Qaradawi, the popular and well-respected religious scholar who has his weekly show on al-Jazeera television, repeat-

edly issued statements justifying "martyrdom operations" as legitimate
jihad against occupiers of Muslim lands in Palestine.[21] Khaled Mishal, the
head of Hamas's political bureau abroad, relies on the authority of these
religious figures to fend off criticisms against suicide bombings. In a television interview with al-Jazeera, he declared that "martyrdom operations are
one of the many forms of resistance; indeed they are the highest and noblest
forms, and most effective. Nearly all of the scholars in our Islamic nations
have ruled that it is permissible and, indeed, one of the best forms of jihad
and resistance."[22]

By refusing to explicitly and unequivocally condemn these attacks
against Israeli civilians, legitimate authority gave radical ideology an opportunity to take root and spread in the Palestinian public. The cultural opportunity that empowered suicidal militants could instead have constrained
their actions. Islam contains strict prohibitions against suicide (verse 4:29)
and prophetic traditions that speak against killing women and children.
Yet religious and government authorities did not attempt to counter the
religious framing of militant groups. The prohibition against killing women
and children falls within a broader prohibition against killing noncombatants in Islam. Verse 2:190 is generally cited as proof of this viewpoint:
"Fight in the path of God those who fight you, but do not transgress limits,
for God does not love transgressors." In my interviews with Hamas supporters, they often argue that it is permissible in Islam to fight enemies in
the same way that they fight you. The fact that Israel kills civilians, they
argue, justifies targeting Israeli civilians. They support their viewpoint by
referring to verse 16:126: "And if you take your turn, then punish with the
like of that with which you were afflicted." However, they neglect to cite
the remaining part of the verse: "But if you show patience, it is certainly
best for the patient." Verse 42:40–43 counsels: "The requital of evil is an
evil similar to it: hence, whoever pardons [his enemy] and makes peace,
his reward rests with God—for, verily, He does not love evildoers. Yet
indeed, as for any who defend themselves after having been wronged—no
blame whatever attaches to them: blame attaches but to those who oppress
[other] people and behave outrageously on earth, offending against all right:
for them is grievous suffering in store! But if one is patient in adversity and
forgives, this is indeed the best resolution of affairs." These verses suggest
that although Muslims are permitted to fight in the same manner in which

they are fought, permission is conditioned by the advice that it is better for the wronged to be patient, and that this is "the best resolution." In the first twelve years of his prophetic mission, Muhammad refrained from attacking his enemies despite their persistent ridicule and persecution. This pacifist stance stemmed partly from the weakness of the nascent Muslim community but also from the desire to protect the emerging creed from charges of overt violence. The Prophet preferred to persuade his opponents rather than fight them. Today the fact that suicide bombings have turned Islam into a fanatical religion in the eyes of the world and in the minds of ordinary observers is lost on those who promote their narrow nationalist causes to the detriment of their religion.

Moreover, many prophetic traditions strictly prohibit the killing of civilians. In one well-known tradition, the Prophet Muhammad is reported to have "once passed by a woman who had been slain. The Messenger of God halted and said: 'She was not one who would have fought.' Then he said to one of [his companions]: 'Catch up with Khalid ibn al-Walid and tell him not to kill women, children and serfs.'"[23] In another report, the Prophet Muhammad said, "You may kill the adults of the unbelievers, but spare their minors—the youth." He also commanded his detachments, "Do not cheat or commit treachery, nor should you mutilate or kill children, women, or old men."[24] According to Rudolph Peters, "All [four Islamic jurisprudence] schools agree that minors and women may not be killed, unless they actually fight against the Moslems."[25]

What all these verses, traditions, and Islamic legal opinions suggest is that the PA and religious authorities had within their possession ample evidence and argumentation to counter the rhetoric of the suicide bombers. Failure to exercise this option made the claims of the radicals appear uncontested and, indeed, definitive.

6

POLICY IMPLICATIONS

uicidal attacks in Russia by Chechen rebels, in Iraq by anticoali-
tion insurgents, in Pakistan against Western and Shia civilians, and
in Saudi Arabia by pro–al Qaeda militants underscore the need
to discover the motivations and conditions for suicide bombings in the
Muslim world. The widespread use of suicidal violence by rebellious
movements—be they religious, secular, nationalist, or ideological—
suggests that governments and societies will have to concern themselves
with this ominous phenomenon for years to come. The attacks of September
11, 2001, the attempted "shoe bombing" of an airliner over the Atlantic,
captured suicide terrorists in Europe, and the bombings in London in July
2005 indicate that this form of terrorism is no longer confined to war-torn
areas such as Sri Lanka, Chechnya, Kashmir, Israel, and Iraq.

This book concerns Palestinian suicide bombers fighting against Israel,
so its conclusions may not extend beyond this case. However, the analytical
framework based on the three levels of analysis—individual motivations,
organizational strategies, and societal developments—could well be useful
to researchers and policymakers seeking to understand the proliferation of
suicide bombings around the globe. The case of Palestinian suicide bombers during the al-Aqsa uprising gives support to the view that, at the level of
the individual, religious and nationalist appeals that equate self-sacrifice with
martyrdom and national salvation are instrumental in producing volunteers
for suicide attacks. Individuals are not inspired to carry out suicide bombings because these are the optimal tactic given the constraints of the political
environment or the calculations of costs versus benefits; rather, they are
inspired by the redemptive nature of self-sacrifice. The religious and nationalist framings of Hamas, Islamic Jihad, and the al-Aqsa Martyrs Brigades
go beyond mere manipulation of individual minds; they combine religious
texts and historical narratives with ritual and ceremony to foster a culture
that venerates martyrdom. The cultural context of Islamic revivalism and
the political context of nationalist conflict allow those appeals to resonate

with the broader public and with potential bombers. Militant groups also draw on the desire for national empowerment in the context of powerlessness in order to motivate individuals to undertake "heroic" acts to shake the passive public into action. Finally, militant groups draw on the desire for vengeance that arises when individuals perceive members of their actual or imagined community as humiliated or traumatized by hated enemies.

At the level of the organization, the case of the Palestinian suicide bombers shows that despite the outwardly religious nature of militant groups, strategic considerations in the context of asymmetrical warfare are the primary drivers for the adoption of suicidal violence as the preferred method of resistance. The difference between those who support suicide bombings and those who oppose them does not correspond to a religious-versus-secular split—both religious and secular factions see the value of suicide attacks. Instead, the split among supporters and opponents corresponds to the divergence between those who believe resistance is the only viable option and those who believe negotiations are more effective. Thus, it would be a mistake to equate suicidal violence solely with Islamism or religious fundamentalism.

At the level of society, the Palestinian case shows that communities embrace and venerate "martyrdom operations" when two conditions converge: (1) communities feel a deep sense of victimization and threat by external enemies in the course of political conflict, and (2) legitimate authorities promote or acquiesce to extreme violence. Palestinian suicide bombings in the al-Aqsa uprising developed out of a mix of threats and opportunities. On the one hand, the Palestinians felt victimized by Israelis who used harsh measures and collective punishments to end the uprising. On the other hand, the Palestinians felt empowered by government and religious authorities to strike back with extreme violence to punish the Israelis. This dynamic suggests that the phenomenon of volunteerism for suicide bombings is intricately connected to the broader political contexts in a given society. Militant organizations, no matter how ideologically savvy and politically astute, cannot generate high rates of volunteerism for suicide attacks without the presence of opportunities and threats in embattled societies.

Analyzing the causes of suicide bombings invariably raises the question, how can we prevent this phenomenon? This question assumes, as this book does, that suicide bombings against civilians are immoral regardless of the circumstances that have given rise to them, or of the strategic advantages that could be derived from them. There are limits—or at least there ought to be—on how aggrieved groups and societies pursue their goals and aspirations; the ends do not justify the means. Moreover, sympathy for a cause, such as the right of Palestinians to live free from occupation, can never justify support for murderous violence against noncombatants. Nor can the atrocities of others, no matter how unjust or egregious, provide the moral foundations for killing innocent people. All three Abrahamic traditions reject the principle of collective responsibility, because it is inherently unjust to punish someone for the misdeeds of others.

In the fight against terrorism, especially this form of extreme violence, the choice is not between good and bad policies; rather, it is a choice between greater and lesser evils. Therefore, every policy recommendation must specify its potential benefits and costs as well as its short-term and long-term implications. Moreover, in confronting suicidal violence we must develop realistic expectations of what can be achieved—military victory is not possible against insurgents who do not fear death, especially when the grievances motivating the violence are legitimate ones with national and international support. We can contain this phenomenon, but we cannot eliminate it without an underlying resolution of the conflicts that generate the rebellions in the first place. Our ultimate goal, therefore, must be an end to festering conflicts that breed hatred and the desire to annihilate the other.

Israel's experience with Palestinian suicide bombers offers many lessons on *how to* and *how not to* deal with campaigns of suicide terrorism. First, Israel's reaction in the first three months of the uprising, characterized by excessive use of force, including lethal bullets, rockets, tanks, and at least two targeted assassinations, escalated the conflict. Selective security measures and military operations to destroy the infrastructure and resources of terrorists are necessary, but when these measures harm the innocent and the guilty alike, they only heighten the legitimacy of suicide bombers. Israel's need to secure its citizens and signal strength in the face of adversaries is understandable, but in the context of armed Palestinian security forces and strong nationalist feelings, Israeli defensive and punitive measures have fostered feelings of victimization and given legitimacy to violent militants who attack civilians. One lesson to draw from this experience is that alternative methods must be deployed to control small-scale violence and riots. Iron-fist policies can result in a backlash that produces more deaths in the long run.[1]

Second, this book questions the view that the organizers of suicide bombings are "enraged fanatics" or "frustrated" souls who are merely lashing out against their enemies. Instead, it argues that they are strategic actors who are conscious of the costs and benefits of different courses of action. This means that they may be susceptible to political and military pressure that raises their costs of pursuing this form of violence. To put it simply, if we are interested in deterring suicidal terrorism, we may have to formulate a strategy that makes this tactic costly to pursue, while simultaneously providing alternative, less costly avenues for these militant organizations to pursue their goals.

Given that suicide bombings are a strategic choice by militant organizations aiming to coerce opponents into making concessions, it would be a mistake to grant major political concessions during a campaign of suicide attacks. Such compromise confirms the viability of this strategy and invites more attacks. The withdrawal of American and multinational forces from Lebanon in 1983 following suicide attacks is often cited by terrorists as proof that suicide bombings can succeed against powerful enemies. In the case of the Palestinians, enthusiasm for suicidal violence during the first two years of the uprising was shaped by a popular miscalculation that Israel would succumb to military pressure and leave the territories in the same way that it left southern Lebanon in May 2000, presumably because of Hezbollah's steadfast armed resistance against Israeli forces during the 1990s. Only after Israel refused to make major concessions and escalated its counterinsurgency against the militants did Palestinian factions begin talking about a cease-fire. As a result of Operation Defensive Shield and subsequent incursions, more and more Palestinians have come to recognize that militarizing the uprising has been a strategic mistake.[2] As one astute Palestinian commentator put it, "When the [al-Aqsa] uprising began, we aspired to liberate the West Bank, Gaza, and Jerusalem. By the end of 2001, our demands regressed to calling for a return to the status quo of September 28, 2000. A little later we lowered our expectations to the point that we are content to return to the conditions on March 29, 2002, the eve of [Israel's Defensive Shield] incursion into the West Bank. [In 2003], none of us aspire[d] to more than having President Arafat left unharmed."[3]

The third lesson is closely related to the second. It is not enough simply to refuse to fulfill the demands of suicidal militants; the authorities must create disincentives for carrying out attacks, by aggressively pursuing the organizers of violence. Given that organizers of suicide bombings calculate costs and benefits of different courses of action and choose suicide bombings because they are effective means to achieving their goals, it would be prudent to raise the costs of militancy in ways that selectively target the militants while avoiding harming civilians. The drawback in this no-concessions and cost-raising strategy is that it polarizes the conflict and intensifies the security dilemma. Militants initially may up the ante in the hope that more pressure will succeed in extracting concessions; the authorities respond with more repression to signal their determination to defeat the terrorists. Tragically, the tipping point for the insurgents becomes apparent only in hindsight.

One way to mitigate this drawback is to offer militants alternative means to resist the occupation. In effect, a carrot-and-stick policy can channel the energy of the militants into less violent means. Israel's persistent military pressure against the militants and refusal to grant them major concessions forced Hamas and other factions to consider a cease-fire in late 2001 and again in 2003. In effect, they were willing to raise the white flag, albeit in the guise of a cease-fire. However, Israel's refusal to accept a mutual cease-fire, and its insistence that the PA dismantle the terrorist infrastructure, negated its cost-raising strategy. Few organizations, no matter how grave the bind in which they find themselves, will agree to surrender their resources and declare defeat without a bitter fight to the end. Put simply, Israel's policy of a stick without a carrot left militant groups no way out other than to exhibit violent defiance. Rather than apply tough security measures to create windows of opportunity for pursuing political initiatives, Israel in effect insisted on an unconditional surrender. Such a victory is not possible against fragmented and decentralized militant groups living among a sympathetic population with national, regional, and international support. While Israel is too strong militarily to be defeated on the battlefield, Hamas and others are too strong politically to be compelled to surrender unconditionally. As a result, until recently, Palestinian factions continued to attack Israel despite their recognition that violence has not achieved its intended aims.

A cease-fire does not yield to the Palestinians either of their strategic goals: a state along the 1967 borders, with East Jerusalem as its capital, and the right of refugees to return to their homes. Therefore, a cease-fire is not a concession that militants could claim as a victory. However, it does create space to pursue negotiations and give the PA an opportunity to entice the factions into agreeing to a permanent cease-fire. Fortunately, it appears that the Palestinians and Israelis have arrived at this conclusion in 2005. To be sure, a cease-fire may give militants an opportunity to reconstitute their cells and build up arms. Negotiations have failed in the past, and nothing guarantees that they will succeed in the future. There is a risk that a cease-fire could be followed by another wave of deadly attacks. These Israeli concerns are legitimate, but given the inability of Israel to completely halt attacks against its citizens after four years of violence, it may be a risk worth taking.

Another lesson from this conflict is that in addition to not giving in to suicide bombings, human intelligence and target hardening can foil the bombers. The more difficult it is to carry out suicide attacks, the more likely insurgents will resort to relatively less costly tactics. Indeed, reports suggest that in 2004 Palestinian militants increased their reliance on mortar and rocket attacks, which are largely ineffective in harming Israelis.[4] Target hardening does not put an end to violence, but it may reduce the casualty rate, because suicide bombings tend to be more lethal than conventional attacks. Securing the homeland through target hardening, setting up checkpoints, and implementing closures reduced the ability of Palestinians to execute suicide bombings. In 2004, 74 percent of suicide attacks were thwarted by the Israelis. It must be said that the motivation to launch suicide attacks has not diminished at all. According to the Israeli General Security Services, in 2004 alone 365 militants were arrested before launching suicide attacks, 46 of them captured at the eleventh hour. That is an average of one thwarted attack per day.[5]

These defensive measures, however, come at a cost. Economically, it is a burden on society to deploy a guard at every bus stop and café; it is not an efficient use of resources. For larger societies, it may not be possible to protect all the vulnerable areas. Morally, human intelligence comes from the use of collaborators who are recruited in suspicious ways and are put in harm's way by the nature of their activities. Politically, checkpoints, incursions, and security barriers have resulted in international criticisms against Israel and have generated additional grievances among Palestinians, which legitimize those who attack Israel. These solutions, therefore, must be viewed as short-term measures to frustrate terrorists and create a window of opportunity for a political process to end the conflict.

So far, the policy recommendations have addressed measures to alter the cost-benefit calculations of organizations and constrain their ability to launch suicide attacks, but what about the culture of martyrdom that facilitates extreme violence? This book shows that the phenomenon of suicide bombings is not simply a security challenge. Suicide bombers and their organizers create cultural symbols that allow them to legitimize this form of extreme violence. Can anything be done to undermine this culture of martyrdom and foster a culture of peace? What role, if any, could the United States and others play in effecting a reversal in cultural attitudes toward suicidal violence?

The culture of martyrdom is inextricably bound to the broader political conflicts that generate polarization and feelings of threat. There is nothing inherent in Islam—or any other religion, for that matter—that inclines people toward death and murderous violence. If there were, suicide bombings would not be such extraordinary events that merit our attention today. The culture of martyrdom is a product of broader struggles that create opportunities for radicals to seek in their cultural heritage symbols, traditions, and rituals to facilitate violent mobilization. Without these conflicts, the culture of martyrdom will wither away. Therefore, in the case of the Palestinians, ending the occupation by giving Israel the peace and security it deserves, and the Palestinians the land and justice they deserve, is the surest way to counter the culture of martyrdom.

The goal of ending the conflict, however, should not relieve the PA and religious figures inside and outside the Palestinian territories of their obligation to debunk the myth of the heroic martyr. Organizers of suicide bombers depend on social legitimacy to recruit human bombs. The PA and religious authorities can raise doubts about the religious acceptability of this tactic as well as affirm Islamic prohibitions against killing women and children in cafés and restaurants and on buses. The PA should insist that there are legitimate means to resist the occupation, and moral lines that should never be crossed. Those who violate these restrictions are not heroes but criminals subject to prosecution.

As for the United States, the European Union, Arab governments, and others concerned with achieving an end to this conflict, they could help in countering the culture of martyrdom by supporting the efforts of Palestinians and Israelis to depolarize the conflict in order to restart negotiations. They could undertake the following measures:

❖ Exhibit their commitment to the peace process by diligently monitoring the cease-fire agreement between Palestinians and Israelis.

❖ Make financial, political, and security aid to the Palestinian Authority conditional on its commitment to negotiations and rejection of violence, ending incitement through the media, and prosecuting violators of the cease-fire.

❖ Make financial, political, and security aid to Israel conditional on its adherence to the cease-fire, cessation of settlement construction, halting of construction of the security barrier/wall of separation, and removal of checkpoints after a period of relative calm.

❖ Offer to take Hamas and other Palestinian factions off the terrorist list, unfreeze their assets, and recognize them as legitimate political organizations if they abide by the cease-fire, that is, end attacks against Israelis, and agree to pursue their objectives through political means.

It is important also to talk about what the United States and other Western powers *must not do* to counter the culture of martyrdom. Attempts to directly influence cultural developments, especially ones bound to religious notions, will undoubtedly be perceived as Western arrogance and meddling in the affairs of others. Not only is this effort difficult to accomplish and rife with pitfalls; it may actually backfire as people interpret such interference as an attack on their creed. For example, calls to reform religious education in Pakistan, Saudi Arabia, and Palestine have led many critics to claim that America wants to "rewrite the Qur'an" or "subvert the will of God." In societies where conspiracy theories have a way of shaping the popular imagination, attempts to urge friendly Middle Eastern regimes and Muslim governments to counter the culture of martyrdom are not likely to yield much fruit, because many of these governments do not hold doctrinal sway over radical Islamists; rather, they are likely to be compromised for doing the bidding of Western powers. The best that Western governments can do is allow this deadly phenomenon to run its course and implode under its own contradictions. Suicide bombings in Palestine have produced only negative consequences. In Iraq, suicide bombings kill more Iraqis than Americans. In Saudi Arabia, suicide bombings have resulted in an outcry against Muslims killing Muslims. If these trends continue, whatever public support there is for such a counterproductive phenomenon will decline. Suicidal violence, in the long run, is tantamount to suicidal politics for those who cannot offer a constructive path to resolving social conflicts.

APPENDICES

Palestinian Suicide Bombings since 1993

	Suicide Bombings in Israel, West Bank, and Gaza (1993–2005)					
Date	Group	Number of Bombers	Number of Victims		Name(s) of Bomber(s)	Age
			Killed	Injured		
09/12/93	Hamas	1	0	2	Aymen Attallah	N/A
09/14/93	Hamas	1	0	0	N/A	N/A
09/26/93	Hamas	1	0	0	Ashraf Mahadi	19
10/04/93	Hamas	1	0	0	Suleyman Zadan	N/A
12/12/93	Islamic Jihad	1	0	1	Anwar Aziz	N/A
04/06/94	Hamas	1	8	44	Raed Abdullah Zakarna	N/A
04/13/94	Hamas	1	5	30	Amar Amarna	N/A
10/19/94	Hamas	1	22	46	Hasan Abd al-Rahman al-Suway	N/A
11/11/94	Islamic Jihad	1	3	12	Hisham Isma'il 'Abd al-Rahman Hamad	N/A
12/24/94	Hamas	1	0	13	Ayman Kamil Radi	N/A
01/22/95	Islamic Jihad	2	21	61	Anwar Sukkar and Salah Shakir	N/A
04/09/95	Islamic Jihad	1	8	30	Khaled Khatib	29
06/25/95	Hamas	1	0	3	Muawiya Ahmed Roka	22
07/24/95	Hamas	1	6	32	Labib Anwar Azem	23
08/21/95	Hamas	1	4	69	Sufian Sbeih Jabarin	26
11/01/95	Islamic Jihad	2	0	11	Ribhi Kahlout, 22; Muhammed Abu Hashem, 18	

		Number of Bombers	Number of Victims		Name(s) of Bomber(s)	Age
Date	Group		Killed	Injured		
02/25/96	Hamas	1	26	0	Majdi Abu Wardeh	19
02/25/96	Hamas	1	1	0	Ibrahim Sarahneh	26
03/03/96	Hamas	1	18	10	Ra'id Sharnubi	N/A
03/04/96	Islamic Jihad	1	12	126	Ramez Obeid	24
03/21/97	Hamas	1	3	48	Musa Ghneimat	28
04/01/97	Islamic Jihad	2	0	3	Abdallah al-Madhoun and Anwar al-Shabrawi	N/A
07/30/97	Hamas	2	16	178	Mouaya Jarara, 23; Bashar Zoualha, 24; Tawfik Yassin, 25;	
09/04/97	Hamas	3	5	181	Yusef Shouli, 23; fifth bomber unknown	
10/29/98	Hamas	1	1	3	Suhib Timraz	19
11/06/98	Islamic Jihad	2	0	24	Youssef Zughayer, 21; Suleiman Tahayneh, 24	
10/26/00	Islamic Jihad	1	0	1	Nabil Arair	24
12/22/00	Islamic Jihad	1	0	5	Hisham Abdallah Najar el Faloji	24
01/01/01	Hamas	1	0	60	Hamed Saleh Abu Hejleh	24
03/04/01	Hamas	1	3	50	Ahmed Omar 'Alayyan	23
03/27/01	Hamas	1	0	27	Dia'a Mohammed Hussein al-Tawill	21
03/28/01	N/A	1	2	0	N/A	N/A
03/28/01	Hamas	1	2	4	Fadi Attalah Yousef 'Amer	23
04/22/01	Hamas	1	1	60	Omar Salem Abu 'Ateiwy	22
04/29/01	Hamas	1	0	0	Jamal Abdel-Ghani Nasser	23
05/18/01	Hamas	1	5	100	Mahmoud Ahmad Marmash	20

Suicide Bombings in Israel, West Bank, and Gaza (1993–2005) (cont.)

			Number of Victims			
Date	**Group**	**Number of Bombers**	**Killed**	**Injured**	**Name(s) of Bomber(s)**	**Age**
05/25/01	Islamic Jihad	2	0	65	Ala Hilal Abdel Satar Sabbah, 19; Osama Nimer Darwish Abu el Heija, 21	
06/01/01	Islamic Jihad and Hamas	1	21	120	Sa'ed al-Hotary	21
06/22/01	Hamas	1	2	1	Ismail al-Masoubi	27
07/10/01	Hamas	1	0	0	Nafez Ayesh al-Nad'ar	26
07/16/01	Islamic Jihad	1	2	11	Nidal Mustafa Ibrahim Abu Shaduf	20
08/04/01	Hamas	1	0	0	N/A	N/A
08/08/01	N/A	1	0	1	N/A	N/A
08/09/01	Hamas and Islamic Jihad	1	15	130	Ezzedin Ahmad al-Masri	23
08/12/01	Islamic Jihad	1	0	21	Mahmoud Baker Nasser	27
09/04/01	Hamas	1	0	20	Ra'ed Nabil al-Barghouti	26
09/09/01	Hamas	1	3	90	Muhammad al-Habashi	48
09/09/01	Islamic Jihad	1	0	17	Abd al-Fatah Muhammad Muslah Rashed	25
10/07/01	Islamic Jihad	1	1	0	Ahmad Abdul Mun'em Ahmad Daraghmeh	17
11/08/01	Hamas	1	0	2	N/A	N/A
11/26/01	Hamas	1	0	2	Taysir Ahmed Ajrami	26
11/29/01	Islamic Jihad	1	3	9	Fares Abu Suleiman	23
12/01/01	Hamas	2	11	188	Osama Mohammed Abed Baher, 23; Mohammed Nabil Jamil Abu Halabiyeh, 25	

Suicide Bombings in Israel, West Bank, and Gaza (1993–2005) (cont.)

			Number of Victims			
Date	Group	Number of Bombers	Killed	Injured	Name(s) of Bomber(s)	Age
					Suicide Bombings in Israel, West Bank, and Gaza (1993–2005) (cont.)	
12/02/01	Hamas	1	15	61	Maher Habashi	21
12/05/01	Islamic Jihad	1	0	8	Daoud Ali Ahmed Abu Sway	43
12/09/01	Islamic Jihad	1	0	30	Nimer Muhammad Yussuf Abu Sayfin	20
12/12/01	N/A	2	0	4	N/A	N/A
01/25/02	Islamic Jihad	1	0	26	Safwat Abdurrahman Khalil	N/A
01/27/02	AMB	1	1	150	Wafa Idris*	20
01/30/02	AMB	1	0	2	Murad Abu Asal	22
02/16/02	PFLP	1	3	30	Sadak Ahad Abdel-Haq	20
02/18/02	AMB	1	1	0	Muhammad Hamuda	N/A
02/27/02	AMB	1	0	5	Dareen Abu Ayshe*	21
03/02/02	AMB	1	10	40	Muhammad Daraghmeh	20
03/05/02	Islamic Jihad	1	1	18	Karim Takhaina	N/A
03/07/02	AMB	1	0	10	Shadi Nasar	24
03/07/02	PFLP	1	0	4	N/A	N/A
03/09/02	Hamas	1	11	54	Fouad Ismail al-Hourani	22
03/17/02	Islamic Jihad	1	0	20	Akram Nabatiti	N/A
03/20/02	Islamic Jihad	1	7	42	Ra'afat Tahsin Slim Diab	20
03/21/02	AMB	1	3	86	Muhammad Hashaika	N/A
03/22/02	Islamic Jihad	1	0	1	Imad Shakirat	N/A
03/26/02	AMB	2	0	0	Shadi Shaker Hamamreh, 22; Khaled Yusuf Dabash, 19	

Date	Group	Number of Bombers	Number of Victims		Name(s) of Bomber(s)	Age
			Killed	Injured		
03/27/02	Hamas	1	28	150	Abed al-Basat Muhammad Ouda	25
03/29/02	AMB	1	2	30	Ayat Akhras*	18
03/30/02	AMB	1	1	30	Muhanad Salahat	23
03/31/02	Hamas	1	15	40	Sh'hadi al-Tubas	23
03/31/02	AMB	1	0	4	Jamil Khalaf Hamid	17
04/01/02	AMB	1	1	2	Rami Muhammad Issa	19
04/02/02	AMB	1	0	0	Akram Khalifa	21
04/10/02	Hamas	1	8	22	Ayman Abu Hajjah	23
04/12/02	AMB	1	6	104	Andaleeb Takataqah*	20
04/19/02	Islamic Jihad	1	0	2	N/A	N/A
05/07/02	Hamas	1	15	60	N/A	N/A
05/19/02	PFLP	1	3	59	Osama Boshkar	19
05/20/02	N/A	1	0	0	N/A	N/A
05/22/02	AMB	1	2	50	Issa Bdeir	16
05/23/02	AMB	1	0	5	Amar Skukani	19
05/27/02	AMB	1	2	37	Jihad Titi	18
06/05/02	Islamic Jihad	1	17	50	Hamza Aref Hassan Samudi	18
06/12/02	AMB	1	1	15	Omar Ziada	30
06/17/02	N/A	1	0	0	N/A	N/A
06/18/02	Hamas	1	19	52	Muhammad Hazza al-Ghoul	22

Suicide Bombings in Israel, West Bank, and Gaza (1993–2005) (cont.)

Suicide Bombings in Israel, West Bank, and Gaza (1993–2005) (cont.)						
Date	Group	Number of Bombers	Number of Victims		Name(s) of Bomber(s)	Age
			Killed	Injured		
06/19/02	AMB	1	7	50	Saed Awadi	17
07/17/02	Islamic Jihad	2	5	40	Mohammed Attala,18; Ibrahim Najie, 19	
07/30/02	AMB	1	0	5	Muhsin Atta	17
08/04/02	Hamas	1	9	40	Jihad Walid Hamada	24
09/18/02	Islamic Jihad	1	1	3	N/A	N/A
09/19/02	Hamas	1	6	59	N/A	N/A
10/10/02	Hamas	1	1	30	Rafik Hamad	31
10/21/02	Islamic Jihad	2	14	42	Hamdi Hasnin, Asraf al-Asmar	N/A
10/27/02	Hamas	1	3	20	Muhammed Kazid al-Bastami	N/A
11/04/02	Islamic Jihad	1	2	69	Nabil Sawalhe	20
11/21/02	Hamas	1	11	50	Nael Abu Hilail	23
01/05/03	AMB	2	23	100	Samer Nouri, 19; Burak Khelfi, 20	
02/19/03	Hamas	1	0	0	Karim Batron	21
03/05/03	N/A	1	17	35	Mahmoud Qawasme	20
03/30/03	Islamic Jihad	1	0	58	Rami Muhammad al-Jameel Ranam	19
04/24/03	AMB	1	1	13	Ahmed Khaled Khatib	18
04/29/03	AMB and Hamas	2	3	60	Asif Mohammed Hanifa, 21; Omar Khan Sharif, 27	
05/17/03	Hamas	1	2	0	Fuad Qaswasmeh	22
05/18/03	Hamas	1	7	20	Bassam Takruri	19
05/18/03	Hamas	1	0	0	Abdel-Fatah Ja'abari	19

Date	Group	Number of Bombers	Number of Victims		Name(s) of Bomber(s)	Age
			Killed	Injured		
05/19/03	Hamas	1	0	3	Shadi Sleyman al-Nabaheen	19
05/19/03	Islamic Jihad and AMB	1	3	70	Hiba Daraghmeh*	19
06/11/03	Hamas	1	17	100	Abd el Muti Shabana	18
06/19/03	Islamic Jihad	1	1	0	Ahmed Abahreh	20
07/07/03	Islamic Jihad	1	1	3	Ahmed Yehiyeh	22
08/12/03	AMB	1	1	10	Islam Yousef Qteishat	17
08/12/03	Hamas	1	1	3	Khamis Ghazi Gerwan	17
08/19/03	Hamas and Islamic Jihad	1	20	128	Raed Abdel-Hamid Masq	29
09/09/03	Hamas	1	8	15	Iyhab Abu Salim, Ramez Abu Salim	N/A
09/09/03	Hamas	1	7	40		
10/04/03	Islamic Jihad	1	21	60	Hanadi Jaradat*	27
10/09/03	N/A	1	0	3	N/A	N/A
11/03/03	AMB	1	0	1	Sabih Abu Saud	16
12/25/03	PFLP	1	4	20	Saad Hanani	18
01/11/04	N/A	1	0	0	Iyad al-Masri	16
01/14/04	Hamas	1	4	12	Reem al-Riyashi*	22
01/29/04	AMB	1	10	50	Ali Jaara	24
02/22/04	AMB	1	8	72	Mohammed Za'ul	23

Suicide Bombings in Israel, West Bank, and Gaza (1993–2005) (cont.)

			Number of Victims			
Date	Group	Number of Bombers	Killed	Injured	Name(s) of Bomber(s)	Age
02/27/04	Islamic Jihad	1	0	0	Abed al-Hameed Khattab	21
03/06/04	Hamas and Islamic Jihad	2	0	0	N/A	N/A
03/13/04	Hamas and AMB	2	10	18	Nabil Ibrahim Masoud and Muhammad Zahil Salem	18
04/17/04	Hamas and AMB	1	1	3	Fadi al-Amoudi	22
05/21/04	PFLP	1	0	5	N/A	N/A
08/31/04	Hamas	2	16	100	Ahmed Qawasmeh, 26; Nassim Subhi Jabari, 20s	
09/14/04	AMB	1	0	3	Yusef Ighbariyeh	22
09/23/04	AMB	1	2	16	Zainab Abu Salem*	19
11/01/04	PFLP	1	3	32	Eli Amer Alfar	16
01/18/05	Hamas	1	1	7	Omar Tabash	21
02/25/05	Islamic Jihad	1	4	50	Abdullah Badran	21

Suicide Bombings in Israel, West Bank, and Gaza (1993–2005) (cont.)

* Female suicide bomber

Selected Wills and Testaments of
Suicide Bombers

Each of the following four wills and testaments was posted on the Web site of the organization that directed the suicide attack shortly after the attack occurred. They have been translated into English by the author.

The Palestinian National Liberation Movement
al-Aqsa Martyrs Brigades
The Will and Testament of the Martyr Mahmoud Siyam

In the Name of God, the Most Gracious, Most Merciful
(Think not of those who are slain in the way of Allah as dead. Nay, they are living. With their Lord they have provision [Q3:169])
The Almighty has spoken the truth.

Praise be to Allah, Lord of the worlds, and peace and blessings upon the most honorable messengers, our Prophet Muhammad, peace be upon him.

I am the living martyr: Mahmoud Saalem Muhammad Siyam—20 years old—the son of al-Aqsa Martyrs Brigades (God willing).

To those who, when their blood is being shed, smile, and when their souls perish, rejoice; to the believers in the age of dissension and the honorable in the age of immorality; to the steadfast in the face of the storm . . . we have no choice but resistance and jihad in the path of God:

I write to you my last will and testament while I am alive, before my martyrdom (God willing). I write it with my tears, not with the ink of my pen. I write it with my tears not out of fear for myself, but in sadness for my mother, whom I urge not to cry when she hears the news of my meeting my Lord. I ask her to rejoice and raise her head high in the sky. O Mother, I know that being nestled in your lap is gentler and kinder on me than my burial grave, but this is God's calling and the calling of my country. For know with certainty that I did not die; I am no longer in an insignificant world that is not worth the wing of an insect, but in a soaring paradise whose fruits hang low, in the company of the God-fearing and the pure, the righteous, the prophets, and the martyrs, God willing.

❖ Dear Father: I urge you to be patient and to pray, for patience is the key to happiness after suffering. . . . I implore you to take the news [of my martyrdom] as any honest believer would, for our reunion is not far off.

❖ Mother . . . Father . . . I urge you to pray and fast . . . to recite and chant the Lord's names, and entreat God to have mercy on me and forgive me; I ask you to be pleased with me and ask God for mercy on my behalf. I know that I will leave a void in your lives, but this is the calling of my God and my nation.

My friends . . . I urge you to stay committed to praying . . . respect God and work with the Holy Quran; fear the Exalted and prepare for the day of departure. . . . For know that a person on the day of resurrection arrives to be judged based on the last words uttered before his death.

I urge you to ask God more and more for forgiveness and repentance, and to make good deeds of your work. I urge you not to defy Him, and to choose the resistance and jihad in the path of God because it is our path for liberation.

For this is jihad . . . victory or martyrdom

[Poem Omitted]

I bid you farewell . . . farewell . . . farewell
I ask you in front of God to forgive me

Your son the living martyr, God willing,
Mahmoud Saalem Siyam (Abu Sihyb)
The son of al-Aqsa Martyrs Brigades

The Palestinian National Liberation Movement
al-Aqsa Martyrs Brigades
The Heroic Martyr Dareen Abu Ayshe

In the Name of God, the Most Gracious, Most Merciful,

Blessings and peace upon the leader of the holy fighters, our Prophet Muhammad, God's blessing and peace upon him:

The Almighty says: So their Lord accepted their prayer, (saying): I will not suffer the work of any worker among you to be lost whether male or female, the one of you being from the other. So those who fled and were driven forth from their homes and persecuted in My way and who fought and were slain, I shall truly remove their evil and make them enter Gardens wherein flow rivers—a reward from Allah. And with Allah is the best reward [Q3:195].

Because the role of the Muslim Palestinian woman is no less important than the role of our fighting brothers, I have decided to be the second female martyr to continue in the path that was forged by the female martyr Wafa al-Idris. I give my humble self in the path of God to avenge the limbs of our martyred brothers and in revenge for the sanctity of our religion and mosques, and in revenge for the sanctity of the al-Aqsa mosque and all of God's places of worship that have been turned into [alcohol] bars in which all that has been forbidden by God is pursued in order to spite our religion and to insult the message of our Prophet.

Because the body and soul are the only things we possess, I give of myself in the path of God to be the bombs that scorch the Zionists, and destroy the myth of God's chosen people.

Because the Muslim Palestinian woman was and continues to take the lead in the procession of jihad against injustice, I call upon my sisters to continue on this path, for this is the path of all those who are free and honorable.

I call upon all who still hold on to an ounce of decency and honor to continue on this road, to make clear to all the Zionist tyrants that they amount to nothing in the face of our determination and our jihad.

Let Sharon the coward know that every Palestinian woman will give birth to an army of living martyrs, even if he tries to kill them in the wombs of their mothers at the checkpoints of death.

The role of the Palestinian woman will no longer be limited to grieving over the death of their husbands, brothers, and fathers; we will transform our bodies into human bombs that spread here and there to demolish the illusion of security for the Israeli people.

In conclusion, I say to every Muslim and determined fighter that loves freedom and martyrdom to stay on this honorable path, the way of martyrdom and liberation.

Your daughter the living martyr: Dareen Muhammad Tawfiq Abu Ayshe

The Islamic Resistance Movement—Hamas
Izzedeen al-Qassam Militias
Will and Testament of the Martyr Muhammad Hazza al-Ghoul
Executed the Jerusalem Operation on Tuesday 18/06/2002

Personal Message

Praise to God who made me one of the sons of Hamas, the movement of unstinting sacrifice, and who made me one of its unique people, one of the sons of the Izzedeen al-Qassam Militias.

How beautiful for the splinters of my bones to be the response that blows up the enemy, not for the love of killing, but so we can live as other people live. . . . We do not sing the songs of death, but recite the hymns of life. . . . We die so that future generations may live.

People of Islam

Do not be fooled by the desperate responses of the unbelievers of this land, for inevitably the circle will close on them no matter how unjust and tyrannical they become, God willing. The triumphant outcome will be to those who fear the Lord, but this will not happen until we champion God and His religion.

Mother, Father, and Honorable Family

I write this testament after I have written two testaments before it, but conditions did not permit the completion of the task until today. I ask God for success, and I ask Him to protect me in His mercy. The martyr intercedes with God on behalf of seventy of his family members, so I request of Him that you be from among them. I ask you, for God's sake, not to cry for my absence, for we will meet shortly in paradise, God willing.

Your son the living martyr,
Muhammad Hazza
18/6/2002
Time 11:45 p.m.

The Islamic Resistance Movement—Hamas
Izzedeen al-Qassam Militias
Will and Testament of the Martyr Hamed Abu Hejleh

{Allah hath purchased of the believers their persons and their goods; for theirs (in return) is the garden (of Paradise): they fight in His cause, and slay and are slain: a promise binding on Him in truth . . . [Q9:111]}

Praise be to Allah, Lord of the worlds, the backer of the holy fighters and the one who humiliates the treacherous Jews. Blessings and peace on the [Prophet Muhammad] head of the believers—the leader of the holy fighters—and on all his family and companions, and all those who follow in his path and strive in his jihad until Judgment Day:

My Loving Family

Rejoice, for I have fulfilled my wish and achieved martyrdom in the path of God with the help of the determined holy fighters. I have left this transient world in a hurry to reach the eternal and everlasting home in paradise, to meet the Prophet [Muhammad], blessing and peace upon him, and the apostles, the saints, the martyrs, and the righteous.

Know that I did not leave you without feeling anguish for missing you, but martyrdom has beckoned me after I had yearned for it for a while. How could I not fulfill this calling, especially when it came to me during Ramadan [the month of fasting], the most blessed month for jihad, martyrdom, and great deeds with God?

Dear Mother

God's contentment with me is dependent on your blessings. My wish [for martyrdom] will not be fulfilled until you are pleased with me. My aspiration will not be complete without your enduring patience, which requires that you consider me a martyr in the eyes of our Lord, a fighter in His path, for the sake of raising His word on earth first and foremost, and for avenging the blood of the martyrs of Palestine. Do not cry for me; instead ululate, for it is the wedding of your martyred son.

Loving Brothers and Sisters

Be supportive of your mother and be from among the patient, the steadfast. Be firm so that you can be helpful of one another. Forgive me if I have done something to offend you. Hold tightly to God's religion and his durable line.

Dear Sister

Accept what I had asked of you before I left you a few days ago to please God, the Munificent. Be alongside your mother and be from among Aisha's [wife of the Prophet Muhammad] sisters and the Khansa [a famous female poet who urged her four sons to fight in the path of Islam and praised God when they were all killed in battle].

To My Honorable Family Members

Forgive me. If I have fallen short in my duty toward you in this world, I will not fall short during Judgment Day, God willing. For know that the Prophet Muhammad, peace be upon him, has said that the martyr intercedes with God on behalf of seventy of his family members. I ask God to give you guidance and goodness.

My Will

My last wish to you my family is that none of you should weep in my procession to heaven. Indeed, distribute dates and ululate in the wedding of martyrdom. I conclude by saying we shall meet soon, God willing, in a paradise prepared for those who fear the Lord, the size of which spans heaven and earth. Lastly, praise be to Allah, Lord of the worlds.

Your son and brother the living martyr,
Hamed Faleh Abu Hejleh

APPENDIX C

Profiles of Palestinian Groups That Deploy Suicide Bombers

HAMAS—ISLAMIC RESISTANCE MOVEMENT (HARKAT AL-MUQAWAMA AL-ISLAMIYYA)

Hamas means "zeal" in Arabic, but it is also the Arabic acronym for the Islamic Resistance Movement. Hamas is a Palestinian political movement with an Islamic orientation. It aims to liberate all of historic Palestine, which today constitutes Israel, the West Bank, and Gaza. Consequently, it rejects peace with Israel and the two-state solution that has been pursued by the Palestine Liberation Organization (PLO) since 1988 and by the Palestinian Authority since 1994. Hamas believes that historic Palestine is an Islamic land or endowment *(waqf)*. Therefore, it is the obligation of every Muslim to liberate this land from the "Zionist usurpers" and all nonbelievers. One cannot negotiate away parts of this land for the sake of peace; Palestine is indivisible.

Hamas emerged in Gaza in December 1987 during the first Palestinian uprising. Its members and leaders came from the Muslim Brotherhood movement that had existed in Palestine since the mid-1940s, before the formation of Israel in 1948. The Muslim Brotherhood was a quietist organization that focused on charity works and proselytizing *(dawa)* Muslims to become more pious. It believed that a successful struggle against Israel was possible only when Muslims returned to their religion, Islam, and upheld their obligations toward God. It was necessary to engender the ideal Muslim individual, family, and society before armed struggle could commence against Israel. Otherwise, the powerful Israeli forces would crush any premature attempts at armed confrontation. The work of the Muslim Brotherhood revolved around three networks: al-Mujama al-Islami (Islamic Center), al-Jamia al-Islamiyya (Islamic Association), and al-Jamiah al-Islamiyya (Islamic University). The first two revolved around mosques that provided services such as medical care, day care, youth sporting activities, *zakat* (alms) collection, and intellectual production; the Islamic University was an academic extension of al-Azhar University in Egypt.

During the early 1980s, the Muslim Brotherhood came under heavy criticism from the Palestinian Islamic Jihad for not participating in the armed struggle, or jihad, against Israel. When the first Palestinian uprising broke out in December 1987, Sheikh Ahmed Yassin, one of the founders of al-Mujama al-Islami and a member of the Muslim Brotherhood, along with other members, felt the need to participate in the popular rebellion that was rapidly spreading to all of the occupied territories. They agreed on the formation of Hamas as a militant political wing of the Muslim Brotherhood. Throughout the first uprising, Hamas produced its own leaflets, organized its own boycotts and strikes, and punished (and later executed) those suspected of collaborating with Israel. To highlight its Islamic orientation and legitimacy, it adopted the following slogan:

> God is our goal *(Allahu ghayatuna)*
> The Prophet is our example *(al-Rasoul qudwatuna)*
> The Qur'an is our constitution *(al-Quran dasturuna)*
> Jihad is our path *(al-Jihad sabiluna)*
> Dying in the path of God is our highest aspiration *(al-Mawtu fi-sabil al-lah asma umniyyana)*

Hamas is keen on separating its political and social activities from its armed ones. Therefore, as early as 1988 it formed an armed wing known as al-Mujahidun al-Falastiniun (The Palestinian Holy Fighters) under the command of Sheikh Salah Shahada. Some of these fighters were drawn from a prior military organization known as Munazamet al-Jihad wal-Dawa or Majed (Jihad and Preaching Organization). The latter was formed in 1986 and was responsible for providing security to the leaders of al-Mujama and punishing known collaborators with Israel. The newly formed armed wing carried out few operations against Israeli targets, but a swift crackdown by Israeli forces in 1989 resulted in its dismantlement.

Hamas's current armed wing is known as Katib al-Shahid Izzedin al-Qassam (The Militias of the Martyr Izzedin al-Qassam). It was formed in Gaza in 1991 and officially unified with the West Bank branch in January 1992. It is named after Sheikh Izzedin al-Qassam, a Syrian-born rebel who fought against the French in Syria in the 1920s and the British in Palestine in the 1930s until he was killed by the British. The task of reconstituting Hamas's military wing in Gaza fell to the young activist Walid Hasan

Ibrahim Aql. He divided Gaza into eight zones and appointed a commander over each zone. Each commander was to form a cell made up of four members. Most of their initial operations targeted collaborators with Israel. They also attempted to use roadside bombs against Israeli patrols, but they quickly abandoned that effort because it was not effective. In the West Bank, the task of recruiting cells fell to Salah al-Arouri, who is believed to have divided the West Bank into seven zones, each with its own commander and cell. Since 1992, Hamas's armed operations, carried out by its military wing, have become more organized and sophisticated. They include armed infiltrations of settlements, armed attacks on Israeli checkpoints, roadside bombs and improvised explosive devices capable of destroying fortified military transport vehicles and some tanks, car bombs, and homemade rockets. Their ultimate weapon, however, is the human bomb.

Palestinian Islamic Jihad (Harakat al-Jihad al-Islami al-Falastini)

The Palestinian Islamic Jihad (PIJ) is also a Palestinian political movement with an Islamic orientation. Like Hamas, it rejects peace with Israel and the two-state solution; liberation of Palestine is an individual obligation (*fard ayn*) on every Muslim. Ideologically, it sees Israel as part and parcel of Western plans to fragment the Muslim nation (*umma*) and keep it subservient to Western interests. Therefore, liberation of Palestine is not merely a nationalist struggle between Arabs and Zionists but also a means to begin breaking the hegemony of the West and subverting Western designs on Muslim lands and resources.

Officially, the PIJ was formed in the early 1980s by Fathi al-Shiqaqi, Abdelaziz Auda, and Bashir Musa. It drew its members from the Muslim Brotherhood, PLO factions, and unaffiliated Palestinians in Israeli jails. The PIJ emerged as an alternative to the secular PLO and the Muslim Brotherhood. It criticized the PLO, arguing that it waged armed struggle without proper religious guidance, and it criticized the Muslim Brotherhood for forsaking armed struggle despite having proper religious guidance. The PIJ combined what it considered the best of both camps: It possessed both religious faith and the determination to engage in armed struggle. These criticisms, of course, no longer applied to Hamas once it adopted armed struggle. The difference between the PIJ and Hamas today is mainly over organizational tactics, not doctrine or strategy. Unlike Hamas, the PIJ does not engage in public welfare activities. Rather, it is concerned mainly with forming a disciplined and secretive organization capable of armed struggle under repressive conditions. It views charity and proselytizing work as a diversion of valuable resources, and ineffective against the existing social order. Only armed struggle will shake off the Israeli occupation of Palestine. Moreover, social activism exposes the organization to undue pressures to compromise its ideological stance and exposes valuable cadres to repression by the authorities.

The Iranian revolution of 1979 played an important role in inspiring the founders of the PIJ to call for the formation of an Islamic organization to lead the struggle against Israel. Secular groups within the PLO relied on Western ideologies and models, failing to appreciate the power of Islam in mobilizing the masses against tyrannical regimes. The Islamic revolution in Iran was able to topple a secular government aligned with the West, thereby depriving the West of control over Iranian resources and politics. Secular nationalism has not been able to achieve similar feats. The PIJ was also inspired by the rise of the Egyptian Islamic Jihad and its assassination of Anwar al-Sadat in 1981. The Egyptian Islamic Jihad was critical of the Egyptian Muslim Brotherhood for failing to take a militant stance in Egypt. Thus, the debates between the PIJ and the Muslim Brotherhood in Palestine mirrored the debates of their brethren in Egypt.

Like Hamas, the PIJ has a military wing, known as Saraya al-Quds (Jerusalem Brigades). These brigades operate in small cells of four or five militants; however, not much is known about their size and geographic divisions. The PIJ has engaged in armed attacks since the early 1980s, but its most spectacular attacks in that decade came in 1987, before the first uprising. The PIJ believes that these attacks set the stage for the first intifada by raising the morale of the Palestinian people as well as showing them the way forward. Since then, the PIJ has engaged in various types of attacks against Israeli targets, including armed infiltrations, car bombings, rocket attacks, and suicide bombings.

AL-AQSA MARTYRS BRIGADES (KATIB SHUHADA AL-AQSA)

The al-Aqsa Martyrs Brigades (AMB) is an umbrella organization consisting of various militias that sprang from the ranks of Fatah, the largest faction in the PLO, and the Palestinian Authority security services. These militias operate in several towns and refugee camps in the West Bank and Gaza, but there does not appear to be an overarching command structure that coordinates the activities of the various militias.

The AMB first emerged as disparate factions with names such as Kateb al-Awda (Returnees Brigades), Kateb al-Shahid Thabet Thabet (the Martyr Thabet Thabet Brigades), and Kataib al-Shahid Marwan Zalloum (the Martyr Marwan Zalloum Brigades). These were not new groups that came out of nowhere or from one specific place. Rather, they were preexisting groups of friends or cadres in Fatah's Tanzim or employees in the PA's security services. Through efforts of local militants in Nablus, Tulkarem, Bethlehem, Jenin, and Hebron, connections were made to merge these groups nominally under the umbrella organization AMB. Sometime in early 2002, Nasser Awais, from the Balata refugee camp in Nablus, was named AMB general field commander over the West Bank. Awais is known to be very close to Marwan Barghouti, who was the general secretary of Fatah in the West Bank, and served as a political liaison between the field and Fatah's leadership, including Yasser Arafat.

Unlike Hamas and Islamic Jihad, the AMB accepts the two-state solution and wants the liberation of the West Bank and Gaza only. Although its rhetoric has increasingly featured Islamic symbolism, its members are known as secular nationalists loyal to Fatah and its late leader, Yasser Arafat. Some analysts contend that the AMB is a rebellion within a rebellion, meaning that its members are of a younger generation that is dissatisfied with the failure of the peace process to achieve its intended aims. More important, they are dissatisfied with the old guard that dominates the top positions in the Palestinian Authority and, consequently, dominates the distribution of patronage in society. They view armed militancy as a way to foster a new legitimacy for themselves and seek to undermine the traditional elites.

Whichever the case, the AMB has emerged as a deadly fighting force capable of planning and perpetrating spectacular attacks against Israeli targets. Although they did not adopt suicide bombings until the second year of the uprising, they have become quite adept at sending human bombs, some of them female. The AMB does not shy away from carrying out joint operations with the PIJ and Hamas.

Popular Front for the Liberation of Palestine (al-Jabha al-Shabiyya li-Tahrir Falastin)

Although the Popular Front for the Liberation of Palestine (PFLP) has carried out fewer suicide attacks in the second Palestinian uprising than the other groups that deploy suicide bombers, it has the longest history of those four groups. The PFLP was founded by George Habash in the late 1960s with a combined orientation of pan-Arab nationalism and Marxism-Leninism. Its aim is to liberate all of historic Palestine and establish a democratic socialist state in its stead. The PFLP joined the PLO in 1968 when it came under the control of Yasser Arafat. However, in 1993 it suspended its participation because the PLO agreed to a two-state solution with Israel.

Similar to the PIJ, the PFLP sees the creation of Israel as an imperialist maneuver intended to weaken the Arab world and keep it divided. Israel is seen as a base of Western colonial ambitions, and its destruction is deemed necessary to weaken Western imperialism in the region. At times the PFLP gave priority to removing what it termed "reactionary" regimes that collaborated with the West, such as that of the late King Hussein of Jordan. The failure of the pan-Arab nationalist movement led the PFLP to innovate in the realm of international terrorism. It pioneered the simultaneous hijacking of airplanes in the late 1960s and 1970s, the most famous episode of which was the September 1970 takeover of two European and two American planes. Three of the planes were forced to land at Dawson Airfield near Amman, Jordan, where the PLO was based at the time. In a daring move, the planes were emptied of passengers and blown up in front of the international media.

Although it was considered the second main faction within the PLO, the PFLP quickly lost ground in Palestinian politics due to the rise of the Islamist factions of Hamas and the PIJ. The failure of Arab nationalism and the collapse of the Communist bloc discredited the twin pillars of the PFLP: nationalism and socialism. The rise of Islamic fundamentalism in the Middle East meant that religious groups were likely to appeal to the sentiments of the masses. Thus, the PFLP plays a marginal role in the Palestinian armed struggle today.

NOTES

INTRODUCTION

1. Joyce E. Salisbury, *Blood of Martyrs: Unintended Consequences of Ancient Violence* (New York: Routledge, 2004); Bernard Lewis, *The Assassins: A Radical Sect in Islam* (New York: Basic Books, 2002); Stephen Frederic Dale, "Religious Suicide in Islamic Asia: Anticolonial Terrorism in India, Indonesia, and the Philippines," *Journal of Conflict Resolution* 3 (March 1988): 38–59.

2. According to Edwin P. Hoyt, *Kamikazes: Suicide Squadrons of World War II* (Springfield, NJ: Burford Books, 1983), 7, suicidal missions were used by the Japanese army in Manchuria during the Russo-Japanese War of 1903.

3. Albert Axell, *Kamikaze: Japan's Suicide Gods* (New York: Longman, 2002).

4. Islamic Jihad is believed to have been a front group for Hezbollah. Martin Kramer, "The Moral Logic of Hizballah," in *Origins of Terrorism: Psychologies, Ideologies, Theologies, States of Mind*, ed. Walter Reich (Washington, DC: Woodrow Wilson Center Press, 1990), 131–57.

5. Ariel Merari, "The Readiness to Kill and Die: Suicidal Terrorism in the Middle East," in *Origins of Terrorism*, 192–210; Hala Jaber, *Hezbollah: Born with a Vengeance* (New York: Columbia University Press, 1997).

6. M. R. N. Swamy, *Tigers of Lanka: From Boys to Guerrillas* (New Delhi: Konark, 1995); Manoj Joshi, "On the Razor's Edge: The Liberation Tigers of Tamil Eelam," *Studies in Conflict and Terrorism* 19 (1996): 19–42.

7. Rohan Gunaratna, "LTTE Child Combatants," *Jane's Intelligence Review*, July 1998; Rohan Gunaratna, "Suicide Terrorism: A Global Threat," *Jane's Intelligence Review*, April 2000; Rohan Gunaratna, "Suicide Terrorism in Sri Lanka and India," in *Countering Suicide Terrorism* (Herzliya, Israel: International Policy Institute for Counter-Terrorism, 2002), 101–108.

8. Christoph Reuter, *My Life Is a Weapon: A Modern History of Suicide Bombing* (Princeton, NJ: Princeton University Press, 2004).

9. Robert Pape, "The Strategic Logic of Suicide Terrorism," *American Political Science Review* 97 (2003): 343–61.

10. Adam Dolnik, "Die and Let Die: Exploring Links between Suicide Terrorism and Terrorist Use of Chemical, Biological, Radiological, and Nuclear Weapons," *Studies in Conflict and Terrorism* 26 (2003): 17–35.

11. On February 25, 2005, Abdullah Badran, a member of the Palestinian Islamic Jihad, blew himself up in Tel Aviv, killing 4 people and wounding more than 50. This attack was seen as an attempt to undermine the efforts of Mahmoud Abbas, the newly elected president of the Palestinian Authority, who was working diligently to secure a formal cease-fire agreement with the armed factions after declaring a truce with Israel's prime minister, Ariel Sharon, on February 8.

12. Two books substantiate this point in other cases, such as the Sri Lankan Tamil Tigers, al-Qaeda terrorists, and Iraqi insurgents. See Mia Bloom, *Dying to Kill: The Allure of Suicide Terror* (New York: Columbia University Press, 2005); and Robert Pape, *Dying to Win: The Strategic Logic of Suicide Terrorism* (New York: Random House, 2005).

1. EXPLANATIONS OF SUICIDE TERRORISM

1. Harvey W. Kushner, "Suicide Bombers: Business as Usual," *Studies in Conflict and Terrorism* 19 (1996): 329–37; Raphael Israeli, *Islamikaze: Manifestations of Islamic Martyrology* (London: Frank Cass, 2003); Shaul Shay, *The Shahids: Islam and Suicide Attacks* (Somerset, NJ: Transaction, 2004).

2. Reuven Paz, "The Islamic Legitimacy of Suicide Terrorism," in *Countering Suicide Terrorism,* 89–98.

3. Anne Speckhard, "Understanding Suicide Terrorism: Countering Human Bombs and Their Senders" (unpublished paper presented at Ideologies of Terrorism workshop, organized by NATO, Brussels, January 31–February 1, 2005).

4. Eyad El-Sarraj, "Suicide Bombers: Dignity, Despair, and the Need of Hope," *Journal of Palestine Studies* 4 (2002): 71–76.

5. Jerrold M. Post, Ehud Sprinzak, and Laurita M. Denny, "The Terrorists in Their Own Words: Interviews with 35 Incarcerated Middle Eastern Terrorists," *Terrorism and Political Violence* 15 (2003): 171–84.

6. Marc Sageman, *Understanding Terror Networks* (Philadelphia: University of Pennsylvania Press, 2004).

7. Ehud Sprinzak, "Rational Fanatics," *Foreign Policy* 120 (September–October 2000): 66–74; Scott Atran, "Genesis of Suicide Terrorism," *Science* 299 (2003): 1534–39.

8. Bruce Hoffman and Gordon McCormick, "Terrorism, Signaling, and Suicide Attack," *Studies in Conflict and Terrorism* 27 (July–August 2004): 243–81.

9. Pape, "The Strategic Logic of Suicide Terrorism," 343.

10. Ivan Strenski makes the point that self-immolation can be viewed as a gift that must be reciprocated by continuing the struggle, which generates a dynamic of autorecruitment for suicide attacks. See his article "Sacrifice, Gift, and the Social Logic of Muslim 'Human Bombers,'" *Terrorism and Political Violence* 15 (2003): 1–34.

11. Mia Bloom, "Palestinian Suicide Bombing: Public Support, Market Share and Outbidding," *Political Science Quarterly* 119 (Spring 2004): 61–88.

12. Eli Berman and David D. Laitin, "Rational Martyrs vs. Hard Targets: Evidence on the Tactical Use of Suicide Attacks," in *Suicide Bombing from an Interdisciplinary*

Perspective, ed. Eva Meyersson Milgrom (Princeton, NJ: Princeton University Press, forthcoming).

2. PALESTINIAN SUICIDE BOMBINGS SINCE 1993

1. The end date of the al-Aqsa Intifada is still uncertain. Although a cease-fire was declared in February 2005 and the level of violence fell substantially in the following months, as of this writing (September 2005) the uprising is not officially over and some attacks continue.

2. Ilene R. Prusher, "As Life Looks Bleaker, Suicide Bombers Get Younger," *Christian Science Monitor,* March 5, 2004; "Palestinian Children: 75 Percent Dream of Carrying Out Martyrdom Operations" (in Arabic), *al-Wasat* (London), January 20, 2003; Eward Cody, "When 'Martyrs' Are Not Yet Men: Palestinians Fear Rise of Youth Suicide Culture," *Washington Post,* May 10, 2002; David Brooks, "The Culture of Martyrdom: How Suicide Bombing Became Not Just a Means but an End," *Atlantic Monthly,* June 2002; Kevin Toolis, "Where Suicide Is a Cult," *The Observer* (London), December 16, 2001.

3. Palestinian Center for Policy and Survey Research, Poll 15, conducted March 10–12, 2005, www.pcpsr.org.

4. Libby Copeland, "Female Suicide Bombers: The New Factor in Mideast's Deadly Equation," *Washington Post,* April 27, 2002; Joel Greenberg, "Portrait of an Angry Young Arab Woman," *New York Times,* March 1, 2002. Hamas employed its first female suicide bomber, Reem Salih al-Riyashi, a married mother of two, on January 14, 2004.

5. Nicole Argo's interviews with fifteen foiled suicide bombers show that one attempted an attack without organizational support, two turned to organizations after failing to secure the necessary logistics for an attack, eight of the fifteen volunteered for an attack rather than being asked to do it, five of the fifteen executed their failed missions within ten days of agreeing to carry out a suicide attack, and seven of the fifteen carried out their failed missions within a month of agreeing to do them. See Argo's forthcoming report "The Istish'hadin," in *Strategic Assessment* (Tel Aviv: Tel Aviv University, Jaffee Center for Strategic Studies, 2005). See also Suzanne Goldenberg, "The Men behind the Suicide Bombers: Every Death Is the Product of a Well-Oiled Killing Machine," *Guardian,* June 12, 2002.

6. Information is derived from two published interviews with Salah Shahada and Muhammad al-Deif, general commander of Hamas's military wing, on Hamas's Web site, www.alqassam.info or www.palestine-info.net/arabic/hamas. See also Nasra Hassan, "An Arsenal of Believers: Talking to the 'Human Bombs,'" *New Yorker,* November 19, 2001; and Cameron W. Barr, "A Suicide Bomber's World," *Christian Science Monitor,* August 14, 2001.

7. According to Hala Jaber, "Inside the World of the Palestinian Suicide Bomber," *Sunday Times,* March 24, 2002, the AMB rejects volunteers less than eighteen years of age, as well as married men with children, anyone without a sibling, and sole breadwinners. They also seek people with steely composure and religiously motivated people "convinced of the meaning of martyrdom." They must also pass as Israeli Jews. During the course of the second uprising, however, the AMB appears to have used children under eighteen years of age to transport explosives and even to carry out suicide attacks.

8. Arnon Regular, "East Jerusalem Cell Opens Window on Hamas Terror Dynamics," *Ha'aretz*, October 2, 2002.

9. Goldenberg, "The Men behind the Suicide Bombers."

10. For a discussion on recruitment of suicide bombers in a comparative perspective, see Ami Pedahzur, *Suicide Terrorism* (Cambridge: Polity Press, forthcoming), ch. 7.

11. Lori Allen, "There Are Many Reasons Why: Suicide Bombers and Martyrs in Palestine," *Middle East Report* 32 (2002): 34–37; Shibley Telhami, "Why Suicide Terrorism Takes Root," *New York Times*, April 4, 2002.

12. Douglas Davis, "Aksa Bombers Educated, Middle-Class," *Jerusalem Post*, March 25, 2002; Hassan, "An Arsenal of Believers."

3. ORGANIZATIONAL MOTIVES

1. Sprinzak, "Rational Fanatics," 66–74.

2. Azet al-Rushuq, "Waqf al-amaliyat al-istishhadiya matlub israeli-amriki ajil" [Cessation of the Martyrdom Operations Is an Urgent Israeli-American Demand], *al-Hayat* (London), May 22, 2002. See similar remarks by Khaled Mishal, head of Hamas's political bureau abroad, in an interview with al-Jazeera, aired during a show titled "Mustaqbal al-Amiliyat al-Istishhadiyya wa Harakat al-Muqawa al-Falastiniyya" [The Future of Martyrdom Operations and Palestinian Resistance Movements], on the program *Bila Hudoud* [Without Limits], hosted by Ahmed Mansour, May 15, 2002.

3. Al-Jazeera television program *Al-Itihaj; al-Mu'akes* [Opposite Direction], August 20, 2002.

4. *Falastin al-Muslima*, "al-Istitan Taraja wa-malyoun Israili Harabou lil-Aysh fi al-Kharaj" [Settlements Are Declining and a Million Israeli Have Fled to Live Abroad], April 2002.

5. *Falastin al-Muslima*, "al-Siyaha Tadharart wal-Numou Taqalas wal-Tajirah al-Kharijiya Tarajat" [Tourism Has Suffered, Growth Has Slowed, and International Trade Has Declined], April 2002.

6. *Falastin al-Muslima*, "Irtifa Halat al-Farar wal-Intihar wa-Asiyan al-Awamer" [The Number of (Military) Desertions, Suicides, and Disobedience of Orders Has Increased], April 2002.

7. Al-Jazeera *Opposite Direction* program hosted by Faisal al-Qasim, "Al-Sulta al-Falastinia wa-Harakat al-Muqawama" [The Palestinian Authority and the Resistance Movements], aired December 18, 2001.

8. Sheikh Ahmed Yassin, founder and leader of Hamas until he was assassinated in March 2004, also rejected the notion that Israeli society contains civilians: "Are there any civilians in Israel? They are all soldiers, men and women, except those religious persons, who do not serve in the army, the rest are all soldiers. The only difference is that they wear civilian clothes when they are in Israel, and military clothes when they come to us. The 20,000 or 30,000 reserve soldiers, where did they come from? Are they not part of the Israeli people? Were they not civilians?" *Al-Hayat*, May 22, 2002.

9. "Battle for the Holy Land," documentary on *Frontline*, PBS, aired May 2002.

10. Ibid.

11. Mohammed Daraghmeh, "Palestinian Militant Group Splinters, Becomes Harder to Rein In," *Associated Press*, November 13, 2002; Khaled Abu Toameh, "Analysis: United They Stand," *Jerusalem Post*, June 9, 2003; Ze'ev Schiff, "Hamas Has Penetrated the Fatah Military Wing," *Ha'aretz*, February 23, 2004; Arnon Regular, "Top Fatah Activists Leaving the Movement to Join Hamas," *Ha'aretz*, March 17, 2004.

12. My analysis of the AMB is based on interviews with Muhammad Daraghmeh, Associated Press journalist covering the Fatah armed groups in the West Bank, on December 12, 2003, in Ramallah; Tayseer Naserallah (Abu Basel), member of Fatah Palestinian National Council, on December 16, 2003, in Nablus; Fayeq Qanan, general secretary of Fatah Movement (Tulkarem), on December 19, 2003, in Tulkarem; and Ghasan al-Hajoui (Abu Hassan), national spokesman for the Prisoners Movement (previously the general director for the Fatah Movement in Megiddo prison), on June 8, 2005, in Haja (near Nablus). I also conducted interviews with officials in the Palestinian Preventive Security Services in Ramallah and with Fatah activists in Nablus and Tulkarem. They did not wish to be cited, for security reasons. See also Human Rights Watch, *Erased in a Moment: Suicide Bombing Attacks against Israeli Civilians* (New York: Human Rights Watch, October 2002).

4. INDIVIDUAL MOTIVES

1. Debra Friedman and Doug McAdam, "Collective Identity and Activism: Networks, Choices, and the Life of a Social Movement," in *Frontiers in Social Movement Theory*, ed. Aldon D. Morris and Carol McClurg Mueller (New Haven, CT: Yale University Press, 1992), 156–73; Bruce Hoffman, "'Holy Terror': The Implications of Terrorism Motivated by a Religious Imperative," *Studies in Conflict and Terrorism* 18 (1995): 271–84; Mara Loveman, "High-Risk Collective Action: Defending Human Rights in Chile, Uruguay, and Argentina," *American Journal of Sociology* 104 (September 1998): 477–525; and Khachig Tololyan, "Cultural Narrative and the Motivation of the Terrorist," in *Inside Terrorist Organizations*, ed. David C. Rapoport (London: Frank Cass, 2001), 217–36.

2. Ann Swidler, "Culture in Action: Symbols and Strategies," *American Sociological Review* 51 (1986): 273–86; Marc Howard Ross, *The Culture of Conflict: Interpretations and Interests in Comparative Perspectives* (New Haven, CT: Yale University Press, 1993); Mustafa Emirbayer and Jeff Goodwin, "Network Analysis, Culture, and the Problem of Agency," *American Journal of Sociology* 99, no. 6 (1994): 1411–54; James M. Jasper, *The Art of Moral Protest: Culture, Biography and Creativity in Social Movements* (Chicago: University of Chicago Press, 1997); Richard L. Wood, "Religious Culture and Political Action," *Sociological Theory* 17, no. 3 (1999): 307–32; Rhys H. Williams and Timothy J. Kubal, "Movement Frames and the Cultural Environment: Resonance, Failure, and the Boundaries of the Legitimate," *Research in Social Movements, Conflicts and Change* 21 (1999): 225–48; Francesca Polletta and James M. Jasper, "Collective Identity and Social Movements," *Annual Review of Sociology* 27 (2001): 283–305; and Rhys H. Williams, "From the 'Beloved Community' to 'Family Values': Religious Language, Symbolic Repertoires, and Democratic Culture," in *Social Movements: Identity, Culture, and the State*, ed. David S. Meyer, Nancy Whittier, and Belinda Robnett (New York: Oxford University Press, 2002), 264–65.

3. Sidney Tarrow, *Power in Movement: Social Movements and Contentious Politics*, 2nd ed. (New York: Cambridge University Press, 1998), 118.

4. A full discussion of the causes and dynamics of Islamic revivalism witnessed since the 1970s is outside the scope of this book. For a good introduction to theories explaining Islamic activism, see Mohammed M. Hafez, *Why Muslims Rebel: Repression and Resistance in the Islamic World* (Boulder, CO: Lynne Rienner, 2003), ch. 1; and Quintan Wiktorowicz, ed., *Islamic Activism: A Social Movement Theory Approach* (Bloomington, IN: Indiana University Press, 2004).

5. Ziad Abu-Amr, *Islamic Fundamentalism in the West Bank and Gaza: Muslim Brotherhood and Islamic Jihad* (Bloomington, IN: Indiana University Press, 1994); Beverly Milton-Edwards, *Islamic Politics in Palestine* (London: I. B. Tauris, 1996); Glenn E. Robinson, *Building a Palestinian State: The Incomplete Revolution* (Bloomington, IN: Indiana University Press, 1997); Shaul Mishal and Avraham Sela, *The Palestinian Hamas* (New York: Columbia University Press, 2000).

6. Sara Roy, "The Transformation of Islamic NGOs in Palestine," *Middle East Report* 214 (Spring 2000): 24–27; International Crisis Group, "Islamic Social Welfare Activism in the Occupied Palestinian Territories: A Legitimate Target?" *ICG Middle East Report* 13 (April 2, 2003): 1–31; Ian Fisher, "Defining Hamas: Roots in Charity and Branches of Violence," *New York Times*, June 16, 2003.

7. From a published interview with Muhammad al-Deif, general commander of Hamas's military wing, on Hamas Web site, www.alqassam.info or www.palestine-info .net/arabic/hamas, March 8, 2004.

8. Published by Ahle Sunnah Wal Jama'at (no publication date or city).

9. See Meir Hatina, *Islam and Salvation in Palestine: The Islamic Jihad Movement* (Tel Aviv: Moshe Dayan Center for Strategic Studies in Tel Aviv University, 2001), ch. 2.

10. Dhafer al-Qasimi, *al-Jihad wal-huquq al-dawliya al-aama fi al-Islam* [Jihad and Universal International Rights in Islam] (Beirut: dar al-ilm lil-malayeen, 1982); Abedi Mehdi and Gary Legenhausen, eds., *Jihad and Shahadat: Struggle and Martyrdom in Islam* (Houston: Institute for Research and Islamic Studies, 1986); Muhammad Shadid, *al-Jihad fi al-Islam* [Holy Struggle in Islam] (Cairo: Dar al-Tawzia wal-Nashr al-Islamiyya, 1989); Keith Lewinstein, "The Revaluation of Martyrdom in Early Islam," in *Sacrificing the Self: Perspectives on Martyrdom and Religion,* ed. Margaret Cormack (New York: Oxford University Press, 2001), 78–91.

11. These prophetic traditions and others concerning the desire to die as a martyr are quoted by Nawaf Hayel al-Takrouri, in *al-Amaliyat al-Istishhadiyya fi Mizan al-Fiqhi* [Martyrdom Operations in Islamic Jurisprudence] (Damascus: Dar al-Fikr, 2003). This book provides justification for suicide attacks and insists that they are legitimate martyrdom operations that can be equated with martyrdom during the time of the Prophet Muhammad. It is advertised on Hamas's Web site, www.palestine-info.net/arabic/hamas.

12. For excellent works that describe the history of persecution, jihad, and martyrdom in the first Islamic community, see Reuven Firestone, *Jihad: The Origin of Holy War in Islam* (New York: Oxford University Press, 1999); Richard Bonney, *Jihad: From Qur'an to bin Laden* (London and New York: Palgrave Macmillan, 2004); and David Cook, *Understanding Jihad* (Berkeley: University of California Press, 2005).

13. See interview with Sheikh Ahmed Yassin in *al-Hayat* (London), May 22, 2002.

14. See interview with James Bennet, "The Bombers," *New York Times,* June 21, 2002.

15. Author's focus on ritual and ceremony was influenced by David Kertzer, *Ritual, Politics and Power* (New Haven, CT: Yale University Press, 1988); and Jack Santino, *Signs of War and Peace: Social Conflict and the Use of Public Symbols in Northern Ireland* (New York: Palgrave, 2001).

16. A recent study confirms that many of the bombers in the Palestinian context come from a religious background or exhibit religious identities. See Leonard Weinberg, Ami Pedahzur, and Daphna Canetti-Nisim, "The Social and Religious Characteristics of Suicide Bombers and Their Victims with Some Additional Comments about the Israeli Public's Reaction," *Terrorism and Political Violence* 15 (Autumn 2003).

17. Read more about her story in Said Ghazali, "The Palestinian Extreme," *The Independent,* May 27, 2003; and James Bennet, "A Scholar of English Who Clung to the Veil," *New York Times,* May 30, 2003.

18. I am indebted to Nicole Argo and Anne Speckhard for conversations and unpublished papers emphasizing the role of trauma and humiliation in the context of community ties. Much of this section is based on their insights.

19. Elizabeth Rubin, "The Most Wanted Palestinian," *New York Times,* June 30, 2002.

20. Benedict Anderson, *Imagined Communities: Reflections on the Origin and Spread of Nationalism* (London and New York: Verso, 1991).

21. Anne Speckhard builds on the notion of fictive kin in "Understanding Suicide Terrorism."

22. Human Rights Watch, "Investigation into the Unlawful Use of Force in the West Bank, Gaza Strip and Northern Israel—October 4 through October 11," *Human Rights Watch Report* 12 (October 2000); www.hrw.org. Human Rights Watch, *Center of the Storm: A Case Study of Human Rights Abuses in Hebron District* (New York: Human Rights Watch, 2001); www.hrw.org. Molly Moore and John Ward Anderson, "Israel Widens Its Range of Reprisals," *Washington Post*, August 7, 2002; Amira Hass, "Deterrents That Haven't Deterred," *Ha'aretz*, August 28, 2002; Reuven Pedatzur, "The Wrong Way to Fight Terrorism," *Ha'aretz*, December 11, 2002; Akiva Eldar, "If Only the Bullets Could Talk," *Ha'aretz*, March 4, 2003; Danny Rubinstein, "Palestinians: Israelis 'Deserved' Haifa Bombing," *Ha'aretz*, March 6, 2003; Gideon Levy, "The Ill Wind Blowing from the Border Police," *Ha'aretz*, May 11, 2003; Danny Rubinstein, "The Point of Control," *Ha'aretz*, May 18, 2003; Amira Hass, "We Don't Raze Homes for No Reason," *Ha'aretz*, June 5, 2003; John Ward Anderson, "Israel's Fence Mixes Security and Politics: As Scope Grows, So Does Hostility," *Washington Post*, September 23, 2003; Akiva Eldar, "What Suffering? The Fabric of Life Is Not Torn," *Ha'aretz*, October 29, 2003; Molly Moore, "Top Israeli Officer Says Tactics Are Backfiring," *Washington Post*, October 31, 2003.

23. Suzanne Goldenberg, "A Mission to Murder: Inside the Minds of the Suicide Bombers," *Guardian* (London), June 11, 2002.

24. All the statements come from John F. Burns, "For Bomber's Parents, a Smile for a Goodbye," *New York Times*, October 7, 2003.

25. Argo, "The Istish'hadin."

5. SOCIETAL MOTIVES

1. Gal Luft, *The Palestinian Security Services: Between Police and Army* (Washington, DC: Washington Institute for Near East Policy, 1998); John Kifner, "Tale of Two Uprisings: This Time, the Palestinians Have Territory, and Guns," *New York Times*, November 18, 2000; Gal Luft, "Palestinian Military Performance and the 2000 Intifada," *Middle East Review of International Affairs* 4 (December 2000): 1–8.

2. Ehud Ya'ari, "Not a Replay," *Jerusalem Report*, November 20, 2000; Salim Timari and Reema Hamami, "Intifadet al-Aqsa: al-Khalfiyya wal-Tashkhis" [Al-Aqsa Uprising: Background and Diagnosis], *Majallat al-Dirasat al-Falastiniyah* 45–46 (Winter–Spring 2001): 7–23.

3. For a Palestinian perspective on possible reasons why the PA played this contradictory role in the first phase of the uprising, see Jamil Hilal, "Intifadat al-Aqsa: al-Ahdaf al-Mubashira wa Muqawimat al-Istimrar" [Al-Aqsa Uprising: Direct Goals and Requirements for Perseverance], *Majallat al-Dirasat al-Falastiniyah* 44 (Autumn 2000): 26–45; Mustapha Barghouti, Saleh Abdel Jawad, Mamdouh Noufal, and Jamil Hilal, "Wajhat Nazar fi Tatawourat al-Intifada wa-Ahdafouha" [Perspectives on the (Al-Aqsa) Intifada and Its Goals], *Majallat al-Dirasat al-Falastiniyah* 47 (Summer 2001): 42–71; and Yezid Sayigh, "Arafat and the Anatomy of a Revolt," *Survival* 43 (Autumn 2001): 47–60.

4. Timari and Hamami, "Intifadet al-Aqsa," 7–23; Mustapha al-Husseini, Yousef Sayigh, Ilyas Shoufani, and Fawaz Traboulsi, "al-Wadh'a al-Filastini al-Rahin wa-Kayfah al-Khorouj Minh" [The Current Palestinian Situation and How to Get Out of It], *Majallat al-Dirasat al-Falastiniyah* 51 (Summer 2002): 7–29.

5. Stuart J. Kaufman, *Modern Hatreds: The Symbolic Politics of Ethnic War* (Ithaca, NY: Cornell University Press, 2001), 31.

6. Leslie Susser, "'We Are Saving Many, Many Lives,'" *Jerusalem Report*, January 15, 2001.

7. See his comments in Khalid Amayreh, "Palestinians Split on 'Armed Intifada,'" al-Jazeera television (Arabic, online), October 19, 2003. www.aljazeera.net.

8. Amnesty International, "Israel and the Occupied Territories: Broken Lives—a Year of Intifada," September 2001, www.amnesty.org. Amos Harel, "No Alternative Found for Crowd Control," *Ha'aretz*, October 1, 2003, and Bradley Burston, "Cries over the Price of a Life," *Ha'aretz*, October 1, 2003, point out that according to an Israeli state comptroller's report, the Israeli Defense Forces did not spend enough money and effort to develop nonlethal weapons to control riots and mass demonstrations before 2000, this despite recognition within the security community of the need to develop new weapons and tactics to control civilian unrest. Part of the explanation for this failure, argues Burston, is that "the military, raised on a model of a force of warriors, resisted efforts to formally redesign their troops as police—despite, or perhaps because of, the months and even years that reservists and conscripts of armored, artillery, infantry and engineers spend on foot patrol and checkpoint duty in the West Bank and the Gaza Strip."

9. Interviews were conducted with Tayseer Naserallah (Abu Basel), member of Fatah and Palestinian National Council, on December 16, 2003, in Nablus; Fayeq Qanan, general secretary of Fatah Movement (Tulkarem), on December 19, 2003, in Tulkarem; and Hussein al-Sheikh, general secretary of Fatah Movement in West Bank (Ramallah), on December 21, 2003, in Ramallah. Tawfiq al-Tirawi, director of Palestinian Intelligence Services, insists that had the Israelis not reacted with such lethal force, events would have turned out differently. See his published interview with the London-based *al-Wasat*, October 13, 2003.

10. Ehud Ya'ari, "Super-Intifada," *Jerusalem Report*, October 23, 2000; Caroline Glick, "Beyond a Reasonable Doubt," *Jerusalem Post*, April 12, 2002; Khaled Abu Toameh, "How the War Began," *Jerusalem Post*, September 19, 2002; Ze'ev Schiff, "Looking Back after Two Years," *Ha'aretz*, September 29, 2002; Greg Myre, "Israel's Case against Arafat," *New York Times*, September 21, 2003; Barry Rubin, "Why Israel's Policy Is Far from Wrong," *Jerusalem Post*, September 23, 2003.

11. Susser, "'We Are Saving Many, Many Lives.'"

12. Khalil Shikaki, "Palestinian Public Opinion and the al Aqsa Intifada," *Strategic Assessment* 5, no. 1 (Jaffee Center for Strategic Studies, Tel Aviv University, June 2002).

13. Jerusalem Media and Communication Center, Poll 41, April 2001, www.jmcc.org.

14. Barry R. Posen, "The Security Dilemma and Ethnic Conflict," in *Nationalism and Ethnic Conflict*, ed. Michael E. Brown (Cambridge, MA: MIT Press, 1993), 103–24; David A. Lake and Donald Rothchild, "Containing Fear," *International Security* 21 (Fall 1996): 41–75; Daniel L. Byman, *Keeping the Peace: Lasting Solutions to Ethnic Conflicts* (Baltimore, MD: Johns Hopkins University Press, 2002); James D. Fearon and David D. Laitin, "Ethnicity, Insurgency, and Civil War," *American Political Science Review* 97 (February 2003): 75–90.

15. Kaufman, *Modern Hatreds*, 32.

16. Daphne Burdman, "Education, Indoctrination, and Incitement: Palestinian Children on Their Way to Martyrdom," *Terrorism and Political Violence* 15 (2003): 102–3.

17. Human Rights Watch, *Erased in a Moment*.

18. In Ramallah during December 2003, the author interviewed a midlevel official in the Palestinian Preventive Security Service who asked to remain unnamed. He confirmed that some militants were taken in order to protect them from Israeli arrests or assassinations, not to control the violence. See also Amnesty International, "Israel and the Occupied Territories and the Palestinian Authority: Killing the Future: Children in the Line of Fire," October 2002, www. amnesty.org.

19. Nawaf Hayel al-Takrouri, in his book *al-Amaliyat al-Istishhadiyya fi Mizan al-Fiqhi* [Martyrdom Operations in Islamic Jurisprudence] (Damascus: Dar al-Fikr, 2003), cites at least thirty-two religious rulings (fatwas) by Islamic scholars around the Muslim world supporting "martyrdom operations" in Palestine.

20. The position of Tantawi on suicide bombings is contradictory and seems to be influenced by his position as a leading authority of Sunni jurisprudence in Egypt, a state that is committed to maintaining peace with Israel and friendship with the United States. In December 2001, he issued a declaration condemning suicide attacks, including those against Israelis (see *al-Quds al-Arabi* [London], December 6, 2001). In April 2002 he said that he approves of "martyrdom" attacks on Israelis, but only against soldiers (see Associated Press, April 14, 2002). A year later he affirmed the right of Palestinians to carry out "martyrdom operations" without explicitly limiting them to soldiers (see al-Jazeera news report, April 5, 2003, www.aljazeera.net). In July 2003 he condemned suicide attacks, even against Israelis, in front of an Islamic scholars' conference in Kuala Lumpur, Malaysia (see "Cleric Condemns Suicide Attacks," *BBC News Online*, July 11, 2003, www.bbc.co.uk).

21. Yussuf al-Qaradawi's weekly program is titled *al-Sharia wal-Haya* [Islamic Law and Life]. His religious rulings regarding "martyrdom operations" aired December 23, 2001, on a show titled "al-Amaliyat al-Istishhadiyya fi Falastin" [Martyrdom Operations in Palestine], and on May 31, 2004, on a show titled "al-Muslimun wal-Unf al-Siyasi" [Muslims and Political Violence]. Yussuf al-Qaradawi's blessing for suicide bombings can be found in interviews with the Kuwaiti weekly *Majallat al-Mujtama'a*, no. 1201 (1996), and the London-based monthly *Falastin al-Muslima*, March 2002. In the latter, he rules that it is permissible for women to engage in suicide bombings. His religious rulings and publications can be found on his Web site, www.qaradawi.net.

22. Interview aired during a show titled "al-Dhahira al-Istishhadiyya" [The Phenomenon of Martyrdom], on the program *Huwar Maftouh* [Open Dialogue], hosted by Ghassan bin Jadou, June 29, 2002.

23. Quoted in Shadid, *al-Jihad*, 149.

24. Quoted in John Kelsay, "Islam and the Distinction between Combatants and Noncombatants," in *Cross, Crescent, and Sword: The Justification and Limitation of War in Western and Islamic Tradition*, ed. James Turner Johnson and John Kelsay (New York: Greenwood, 1990), 199.

25. Rudolph Peters, *Islam and Colonialism: The Doctrine of Jihad in Modern History* (The Hague: Mouton, 1979), 21.

6. Policy Implications

1. Some Israeli analysts have come to this conclusion. See Ze'ev Schiff, "Qassams Symbolize a Failure to Deter," *Ha'aretz*, May 20, 2003; Uzi Benziman, "Corridors of Power: When the Bubbles Burst," *Ha'aretz*, May 23, 2003; and Doron Rosenblum, "No Success Like Failure," *Ha'aretz*, September 12, 2003.

2. Gideon Alon and Amira Hass, "IDF: Voices Growing in Fatah for End to Suicide Attacks," *Ha'aretz*, August 13, 2002; Khaled Abu Toameh, "Arafat's Economic Adviser Calls for Cease-Fire," *Jerusalem Post*, December 5, 2002; Danny Rubinstein, "Nonviolence: Why Didn't We Think of That Before?" *Ha'aretz*, August 3, 2003.

3. Wahid Abdelmajid, "al-Intifada al-Falastiniya Bayn Khayari al-Murajaa wal-Tarajua" [The Uprising between Two Options: Rethinking or Retreat], *al-Hayat*, October 8, 2002. See similar remarks by Nabil Amr, former minister of information in the Palestinian Authority, in Khalid Amayreh, "Palestinians Split on 'Armed Intifada,'" al-Jazeera, October 19, 2003, www.aljazeera.net.

4. The Israeli General Security Services reported that in 2004 alone Palestinian factions fired approximately 1,540 mortar and rocket rounds against Israeli targets. Haim Shibi, "Toll of Blood: The Intifada in Numbers," *Yedioth Ahronoth*, January 5, 2005.

5. Ibid.

RESOURCES FOR FURTHER RESEARCH

BOOKS

Abu-Amr, Ziad. *Islamic Fundamentalism in the West Bank and Gaza: Muslim Brotherhood and Islamic Jihad.* Bloomington, IN: Indiana University Press, 1994.

Axell, Albert, and Hideaki Kase. *Kamikaze: Japan's Suicide Gods.* New York: Longman, 2002.

Bloom, Mia. *Dying to Kill: The Allure of Suicide Terror.* New York: Columbia University Press, 2005.

Gambetta, Diego, ed. *Making Sense of Suicide Missions.* New York: Oxford University Press, 2005.

Harik, Judith Palmer. *Hezbollah: The Changing Face of Terrorism* London: I. B. Tauris, 2004.

Hatina, Meir. *Islam and Salvation in Palestine: The Islamic Jihad Movement.* Tel Aviv: Dayan Center Papers 127, 2001.

Hroub, Khaled. *Hamas: Political Thought and Practice.* Washington, DC: Institute for Palestine Studies, 2000.

Human Rights Watch. *Erased in a Moment: Suicide Bombing Attacks against Israeli Civilians* (New York: Human Rights Watch, 2002).

Inoguchi, Rikihei, and Tadashi Nakajima. *The Divine Wind: Japan's Kamikaze Force in World War II.* Annapolis, MD: Naval Institute Press, 1958.

Jaber, Hala. *Hezbollah.* New York: Columbia University Press, 1997.

Khosrokhavar, Farhad. *Suicide Bombers: Allah's New Martyrs.* London: Pluto Press, 2005.

Oliver, Anne Marie, and Paul Steinberg. *The Road to Martyrs' Square: A Journey into the World of the Suicide Bomber.* New York: Oxford University Press, 2004.

Mishal, Shaul, and Avraham Sela. *The Palestinian Hamas.* New York: Columbia University Press, 2000.

Pape, Robert. *Dying to Win: The Strategic Logic of Suicide Terrorism.* New York: Random House, 2005.

Pedahzur, Ami. *Suicide Terrorism.* Cambridge: Polity, 2005.

Reuter, Christoph. *My Life Is a Weapon: A Modern History of Suicide Bombing.* Princeton, NJ: Princeton University Press, 2004.

ARTICLES

Andoni, Lamis. "Searching for Answers: Gaza's Suicide Bombers." *Journal of Palestine Studies* 26, no. 4 (Summer 1997): 33–46.

Atran, Scott. "Genesis of Suicide Terrorism." *Science* 299 (2003): 1534–39.

Dale, Stephen Frederic. "Religious Suicide in Islamic Asia: Anticolonial Terrorism in India, Indonesia, and the Philippines." *Journal of Conflict Resolution* 3 (March 1988): 38–59.

Gunaratna, Rohan. "Suicide Terrorism: A Global Threat." *Jane's Intelligence Review* 12 (April 2000).

———. "Suicide Terrorism in Sri Lanka and India." *Countering Suicide Terrorism* (2002): 101–8.

Hassan, Nasra. "An Arsenal of Believers: Talking to the 'Human Bombs.'" *New Yorker*, November 19, 2001.

Hoffman, Bruce, and Gordon McCormick. "Terrorism, Signaling, and Suicide Attack." *Studies in Conflict and Terrorism* 27, no. 4 (July–August 2004): 243–81.

Kushner, Harvey W. "Suicide Bombers: Business as Usual." *Studies in Conflict and Terrorism* 19 (1996): 329–37.

Merari, Ariel. "The Readiness to Kill and Die: Suicidal Terrorism in the Middle East." In *Origins of Terrorism: Psychologies, Ideologies, Theologies, States of Mind,* edited by Walter Reich, 192–210. Washington, DC: Woodrow Wilson Center Press, 1990.

Moghadam, Assaf. "Palestinian Suicide Terrorism in the Second Intifada: Motivations and Organizational Aspects." *Studies in Conflict and Terrorism* 26 (2003): 65–92.

Pape, Robert. "The Strategic Logic of Suicide Terrorism." *American Political Science Review* 97 (2003): 343–61.

Sprinzak, Ehud. "Rational Fanatics." *Foreign Policy* 120 (September–October 2000): 66–74.

DOCUMENTARIES

❖ *The Bombing.* First Run/Icarus Films, 1999.

❖ *The Living Martyr: Inside the Hezbollah.* Films for the Humanities and Social Sciences, 2000.

❖ *Inside the Mind of a Suicide Bomber.* The History Channel, 2001.

❖ "Shattered Dreams of Peace: The Road from Oslo." PBS, *Frontline,* 2002.

❖ "Battle for the Holy Land." PBS, *Frontline,* 2002.

❖ *Human Weapon.* First Run/Icarus Films, 2002.

❖ "Suicide Bombers." PBS, *Wide Angle,* 2004.

❖ "Female Suicide Bombers." *National Geographic Explorer,* special edition, 2004.

Index

Names beginning with "al-" or "el" are alphabetized under the next word in the name. Page numbers in *italic* indicate charts or tables.

ABOUT THE AUTHOR

Mohammed M. Hafez is a visiting professor in the Department of Political Science at the University of Missouri, Kansas City. He earned a BA in political science from the University of California, Los Angeles, an MA in international relations from the University of Southern California, and a PhD in international relations from the London School of Economics and Political Science. Hafez was a Harry Frank Guggenheim Foundation fellow and a United States Information Agency fellow during 1998–99. He wrote the book *Why Muslims Rebel: Repression and Resistance in the Islamic World* (2003) and teaches courses on Islam and world politics, the politics of the Middle East, religion and politics, terrorism and political violence, and the Arab-Israeli conflict. His research on suicide bombers has been presented in conferences hosted by the National Institute of Justice, the U.S. Department of State, the Center for Naval Analysis, and NATO.